The Bedford Glossary
for U.S. History

The Bedford Glossary
for U.S. History

Marion Menzin

Harvard University

Courtney Podraza

Harvard University

Shawn Alexander

Yale University

Bedford/St. Martin's
Boston ◆ New York

For Bedford/St. Martin's

Executive Editor for History: Mary V. Dougherty
Director of Development for History: Jane Knetzger
Developmental Editor: Shannon Hunt
Production Editor: Amy Derjue
Projection Supervisor: Matthew Hayes
Senior Marketing Manager: Jenna Bookin Barry
Copyeditor: Lisa Wehrle
Cover Design: Billy Boardman
Composition: DeNee Reiton Skipper
Printing and Binding: Malloy Lithographing, Inc.

President: Joan E. Feinberg
Editorial Director: Denise B. Wydra
Director of Marketing: Karen Melton Soeltz
Director of Edition, Design and Production: Marcia Cohen

Library of Congress Control Number: 2006900742

Manufactured in the United States of America.

9 8 7
o n m l

For information, write: Bedford/St. Martin's, 75 Arlington Street, Boston, MA 02116
(617-399-4000)

ISBN: 0–312–45144–X
EAN: 978–0–312–45144–8

Preface

The Bedford Glossary for U.S. History offers students clear, concise definitions of terms commonly used by both historians and political commentators. This portable volume contains vocabulary that students will encounter in their reading for the course as well as in contemporary media, enabling them to participate knowledgeably in discussions inside and outside the classroom. The terms are arranged alphabetically and cover political, economic, social, and cultural topics as well as prominent court cases. Definitions provide a time period and historical context to help students locate the term in U.S. history and comprehend its significance. Incorporating and expanding on the glossaries found in Bedford/St. Martin's introductory U.S. history survey texts—*The American Promise*, by James L. Roark, Michael P. Johnson, Patricia Cline Cohen, Sarah Stage, Alan Lawson, and Susan M. Hartmann; and America's History, by James A. Henretta, David Brody, and Lynn Dumenil—*The Bedford Glossary for U.S. History* serves as a handy supplement for both the complete and concise versions of these books.

Acknowledgments

Thanks go to the following reviewers of *The Bedford Glossary for U.S. History,* whose thoughtful comments were of great help in the development of this volume: Randal Beeman, Bakersfield College; Susan Edwards, Cy-Fair College; Maurine Greenwald, University of Pittsburgh; David Howard-Pitney, De Anza College; and Terry M. Thomas, Austin Community College.

The Bedford Glossary
for U.S. History

A

abolitionism The social reform movement to end slavery and the slave trade that began in the late eighteenth century. Abolitionists held a variety of ideological convictions: Some advocated for sending ex-slaves back to Africa or to a settlement in Canada; others promoted a racially integrated society in which blacks would be treated as equals to whites. Abolitionism gained momentum in the 1830s with the rise of antislavery societies and newspapers in the northern states. While many northerners disapproved of slavery, they did not all join the abolition cause because they viewed blacks as inferiors. The geographic expansion of the nation during the 1840s offered abolitionists an opportunity to link their antislavery activism to a goal that many white northerners found much more attractive—limiting the geographic expansion of slavery. Slavery officially ended after the Civil War (1861–1865) with the passage of the Thirteenth Amendment in 1865.

affirmative action Policies established in the 1960s and 1970s by governments, businesses, universities, and other institutions to overcome the effects of past discrimination against specific groups such as racial and ethnic minorities and women. Measures to ensure equal opportunity include setting goals for the admission, hiring, and promotion of minorities; considering minority status when allocating resources; and actively encouraging victims of past discrimination to apply for jobs and other resources.

AFL-CIO *See* American Federation of Labor-Congress of Industrial Organizations.

agribusiness Farming on a large scale, using the production, processing, and distribution methods of modern business. As farms grew larger and more mechanized in the late nineteenth century, farming became a big business, not just a means of feeding a family and making a living. In the 1940s and 1950s, specialized commercial farms replaced many family-run operations.

AIM *See* American Indian Movement.

alien A person who is not a citizen or national of the country in which he or she is living. The United States recognizes two kinds of aliens: temporary visitors, who are registered as visitors and cannot travel or accept employment without permission;

and resident aliens, who live in the United States on a permanent basis and hold the basic rights of citizens but cannot vote or hold public office. The U.S. government first registered aliens in 1940. Illegal aliens are noncitizens living in the country without proper documentation who can be deported if detected.

Alien and Sedition Acts Laws passed by the new U.S. government in 1798 that restricted the rights of immigrants and criminalized criticism of the president or Congress. The acts reflected concerns about political instability and the danger of war with France. Though the Alien and Sedition Acts expired in 1802, the government's struggle to balance the need for security with individual rights continues to the present day.

alliance system The military and diplomatic system formulated in an effort to create a balance of power in pre–World War I Europe. Certain European nations were bound together by rigid and comprehensive treaties that promised mutual aid to allies in the case of attack. The system swung into action after the Austrian archduke Franz Ferdinand was assassinated in Sarajevo on June 28, 1914, dragging most of Europe into World War I (1914–1918).

alphabet soup agencies The nickname for the vast number of New Deal agencies that were usually referred to by their initial letters, for example, the AAA (Agricultural Adjustment Association), CCC (Civilian Conservation Corps), NRA (National Recovery Administration), and TVA (Tennessee Valley Authority). *See also* New Deal.

America First Committee A committee organized by isolationists in 1940 to oppose the entrance of the United States into World War II (1939–1945). The membership of the committee included senators, journalists, and publishers. Perhaps the most well-known member was the aviator Charles Lindbergh.

American Federation of Labor-Congress of Industrial Organizations (AFL-CIO) The largest federation of labor unions in the United States, formed in 1955 with the merger of the American Federation of Labor and the Congress of Industrial Organizations. The AFL-CIO generally has focused on "bread-and-butter" issues, working with corporations to provide workers with better hours, pay, and benefits.

American Indian Movement (AIM) A civil rights organization founded in 1968 that works for the civil rights and improved living conditions of Native Americans. AIM has been critical of the federal Bureau of Indian Affairs, which it believes has failed to address the widespread poverty, joblessness, and housing discrimination among Native Americans. Since its inception, AIM has staged several protests to call attention to the problems of American Indians. In 1972, members occupied the Bureau of Indian Affairs for several days, and in 1973, AIM members and other American Indians seized Wounded Knee, South Dakota, where the U.S. Cavalry massacred as many as three hundred Sioux in 1890.

American Lyceum A lecture circuit beginning in 1826 that sent ministers, transcendentalists, and scientists all across the North on speaking tours. The Lyceum movement helped to spread transcendentalism and reform ideas in the nineteenth century. *See also* transcendentalism.

American System A government program conceived in the early 1820s to expand economic development through a federally funded system of internal improvements (roads and canals), tariffs, and a national bank. Such policies marked a shift toward government involvement in the economy, reflecting the growing strength of commercial interests.

anarchism A philosophy advocating the revolutionary creation of a stateless society. Anarchists believe that government of any kind is unnecessary and undesirable and should be replaced with voluntary cooperation and free association. Anarchists became increasingly visible in the United States in the late nineteenth and early twentieth centuries. They advocated revolution and grew in numbers through appeals to discontented laborers, leading immigrant anarchists to become reviled as foreign corruptors of the American worker.

Anglican Church *See* Church of England.

Anglo-Saxonism A theory that the English, and by extension their American cousins, were successful because of racial superiority. Combined with social Darwinism, this notion fueled westward expansion in the late nineteenth century.

antebellum Latin for "before a war"; commonly used by historians to refer to the period prior to the Civil War (1861–1865).

Antifederalists Opponents of the Constitution who argued against the new plan of government proposed in 1787. Antifederalists believed that the Constitution would diminish the power of the states, create a new merchant-based aristocracy, and, without a declaration of individual rights, threaten personal liberties. They also believed that republican institutions of government would not function in a territory as large as the United States.

antilynching movement A late-nineteenth-century campaign to make the act of lynching, execution by a mob without legal sanction, a federal crime. This movement, led by reporter Ida B. Wells, was part of the larger progressive movement to reform U.S. society and government. *See also* lynching.

antinomian A person who does not obey societal or religious law. In colonial Massachusetts, Puritan authorities labeled Anne Hutchinson an antinomian, accusing her of believing that Christians did not necessarily need to act in accordance with God's law or the laws of the Massachusetts Bay Colony but could achieve salvation by faith alone.

anti-Semitism *See* Judaism.

antitrust The prevention of large business mergers or corporate structures that may interfere with economic competition or encourage price-fixing. In 1890, the U.S. government passed the Sherman Antitrust Act and, in 1914, bolstered the act by passing two additional antitrust laws. In 1998, the U.S. Justice Department and a number of state attorneys general filed an antitrust lawsuit against Microsoft Corporation.

appeasement Pacifying an enemy by making concessions. In the context of World War II (1939–1945), it refers specifically to the 1938 agreement reached at Munich, Germany, when England and France agreed to allow Adolf Hitler to annex the Sudetenland (part of the current Czech Republic) in exchange for his promise not to take more territory. After World War II, many politicians disparaged appeasement as a ruinous diplomatic strategy.

archaeology A social science devoted to learning about people who lived in the past through the study of physical artifacts created by humans. Most but not all archaeological study focuses on the history of people who lived before the use of the written word.

Archaic America The period of time (roughly from 10,000 BP to between 4000 and 3000 BP) when various hunting and gathering cultures descended from Paleo-Indians dominated ancient America. *See also* Paleo-Indians.

Arminianism A Protestant religious movement founded in the early 1600s by Dutch theologian Jacobus Arminius. Arminius taught that people's good deeds could help their chances of salvation, which contradicted the Puritan's Calvinist beliefs. In the 1630s, Puritan Anne Hutchinson accused ministers of the Massachusetts Bay Colony of preaching Arminian ideas. Arminianism influenced Methodism as well as other Protestant denominations. *See also* Calvinism, Methodism.

armistice The equivalent of a cease-fire during which peace negotiations take place. During the armistice following World War I (1914–1918), nations from around the world sent diplomats to the Paris peace conference, although most of the negotiations were handled by the United States, France, and Great Britain.

arms race A military rivalry between two or more countries to maintain an equal or greater stockpile of weapons than competitors. In the second half of the twentieth century, the United States and the Soviet Union both acquired large stores of nuclear weapons in an effort to deter each other's governments from attacking.

Articles of Confederation A document finalized in 1777 that articulated the powers of the Second Continental Congress. It preserved states' rights while authorizing a limited central government—the Congress—with power to defend the Union and conduct foreign affairs. Since it allowed for no taxation, executive (president), or national judiciary, the Articles left the Congress too weak to carry out even its limited duties. It was replaced by the Constitution in 1787.

artifacts Material remains studied and used by archaeologists and historians to support their interpretations of human history. Examples of artifacts include bones, pots, baskets, jewelry, furniture, tools, clothing, and buildings.

artisan A skilled craftsperson, such as a cabinetmaker. As unskilled factory labor became increasingly common in the late nineteenth and early twentieth centuries, the artisan worker largely disappeared.

assimilation The absorption of dominant cultural values and customs by a minority group. Immigrant groups throughout U.S. history have struggled with pressures to assimilate into U.S. society.

assumption The proposal by Alexander Hamilton in 1790 that the new federal government take on the states' foreign debts to improve the country's credit. Though it eventually prevailed, this proposal was highly controversial, and not just because it placed an unfair burden on states that had already paid their debts. Assumption raised concerns about the growing involvement of the federal government in the U.S. economy.

Atlantic World The society created by political, cultural, and economic exchanges between people in Europe, Africa, and the Americas during the colonial period. In recent years, historians have emphasized the importance of trans-Atlantic connections in understanding colonial societies.

B

baby boom A period of increased birthrates during a time of economic prosperity. The United States experienced a baby boom following World War II (1939–1945) that lasted from 1946 until the early 1960s.

Back to Africa Movement A movement led by black nationalist Marcus Garvey to promote the migration of African Americans to Africa after World War I (1914–1918). The Back to Africa Movement emerged in reaction to white racism and the perceived accommodation of organizations such as the National Association for the Advancement of Colored People to the existing racial hierarchy. Garvey was the leader of the Universal Negro Improvement Association, which encouraged blacks to become entirely independent from white society.

bank holiday State or federal government closure of lending institutions to prevent their going broke. The use of this euphemism by President Franklin D. Roosevelt (1933–1945) during the Great Depression was an attempt to put a positive face on an unpleasant reality.

Baptist An evangelical religious denomination that spread during the late eighteenth and early nineteenth centuries, known for its emphasis on fervent conversion experiences, a baptism by full immersion in water, and inclusion of women and slaves. In the twenty-first century, the Southern Baptists form the largest Protestant denomination in the United States, claiming about 16 million members.

Beat generation A small group of literary figures based in New York City and San Francisco in the 1950s who rejected mainstream culture and instead celebrated personal freedom, which often included drug consumption and casual sex. Their rebelliousness provided a model for the much larger movement of youthful dissidents in the 1960s.

Benevolent Empire A broad-ranging campaign of moral and institutional reform inspired by evangelical Christian ideals and created by middle-class men and women in the 1820s. "Benevolence" became a seminal concept in American spiritual thinking during the Second Great Awakening. Promoters of benevolent reform suggested that people who had experienced God's saving grace should provide charity to the less fortunate.

Bering land bridge The piece of land (now under water) that connected Asia with North America, exposed many thousands of years ago during a global ice age. The Bering land bridge enabled nomadic hunters and gatherers to make their way into the previously uninhabited continent of North America. These settlers were the ancestors of the American Indians.

bicameral legislature A two-house assembly, usually a house of representatives and a senate, suggested by John Adams in his *Thoughts on Government* (1776). Different qualifications, procedures, term lengths, and means of election differentiate the two. A bicameral legislative system ensures that each piece of legislation is reviewed and debated by two independent groups.

Bill of Rights The first ten amendments to the U.S. Constitution. The Bill of Rights (the last of which was ratified in 1791) guarantees individual liberties and defines limitations to federal power. Many states made the promise of the prompt addition of a bill of rights a precondition for their ratification of the Constitution.

bills of exchange Credit slips that British manufacturers, West Indian planters, and American merchants used to trade among themselves in the eighteenth century.

black codes Laws passed by the southern states after the Civil War (1861–1865) to limit the economic, political, and civil rights of African Americans. Such repression continued until the civil rights movement of the mid-twentieth century.

black nationalism Theory adopted by several African American movements that emphasized racial pride, separation from whites and white institutions, and black autonomy. Black nationalism gained in popularity with the rise of Marcus Garvey and the Universal Negro Improvement Association and later with the Black Panther Party, Malcolm X, and other participants of the black power movements of the 1960s.

black power *See* black nationalism.

blacklist Procedure used by employers to label and identify undesirable workers. Blacklisting, often of innocent people, was common during the anti-Communist hysteria of the 1940s and 1950s.

Bleeding Kansas Reference to the violence that erupted in Kansas in 1855 and 1856 over slavery. The Kansas-Nebraska Act of 1854 allowed settlers to decide whether to allow slavery within the territory's borders. Proslavery and abolitionist groups across the country battled over Kansas as a symbol of America's future status as a slave or free nation.

blitzkrieg German for "lightning war"; the tactics employed by the Germans in 1939–1940 when they used massed armored and air forces to overrun Poland and the countries of Western Europe.

bloody shirt A refrain used by Republicans in the late nineteenth century to remind the voting public that the Democratic Party, dominated by the South, was largely responsible for the Civil War (1861–1865) and that the Republican Party had led the victory to preserve the Union. Republicans urged their constituents to "Vote the way you shot."

blue collar A worker employed in manual or technical labor. The term originally referred to workplace dress codes in the late nineteenth and early twentieth centuries. Industrial or factory workers traditionally wore blue work shirts.

blue laws The legal restriction of activity on Sundays. In the late nineteenth century, Sunday closings of businesses were encouraged by Protestants as part of their crusade to uphold social values, leaving the day free for worship, but these closings were considered by immigrant Catholics as a violation of their personal freedom.

bolshevism The original term for Russian communism. Bolsheviks, led by Vladimir Lenin, seized power in Russia in 1917. *See also* communism.

boomtowns Mid- to late-nineteenth-century frontier settlements created virtually overnight following the news of a gold strike. A high ratio of men to women and a transient population added to their rough-and-tumble atmosphere.

boycott The strategy of refusing to buy, sell, or trade with a person, company, or government as a protest of a policy or action. Americans have frequently used boycotts to push for social and political changes. Colonists boycotted British products before the American Revolution (1775–1783) and African Americans have used the strategy against discriminatory businesses since the Civil War (1861–1865). The Montgomery bus boycott

(1955–1956), led by Martin Luther King Jr., helped launch the direct action campaigns of the civil rights movement.

***bracero* program**   Begun during World War II (1939–1945) to help with wartime agriculture, this federal program permitted Mexican laborers (*braceros* in Spanish) to enter the United States and work for a limited period of time but not to gain citizenship or permanent residence. The program officially ended in 1964.

brinksmanship   A cold war practice of appearing willing and able to resort to nuclear war in order to make an enemy back down. Secretary of State John Foster Dulles, under President Dwight D. Eisenhower (1953–1961), was the foremost proponent of this policy.

broad constructionism   *See* strict constructionism.

Brown v. Board of Education   A unanimously decided 1954 Supreme Court case that outlawed the "separate but equal" educational facilities for blacks and whites across the South, declared segregation a violation of the Fourteenth Amendment, and set the precedent upon which government-sanctioned segregation could be banned. In 1950, the families of eight Topeka, Kansas, children sued the Topeka Board of Education. The children lived within walking distance of a whites-only school but were instead forced to take an inconvenient and dangerous route to get to a black school. Their parents argued that their children should be allowed to attend the nearest school. By the time the case reached the Supreme Court, it had been joined with similar cases of segregated schools in other states and the District of Columbia. A team of lawyers from the National Association for the Advancement of Colored People urged the Court to overturn the fifty-eight-year-old precedent established in *Plessy v. Ferguson*, which had enshrined "separate but equal" as the law of the land. *See also Plessy v. Ferguson.*

buffalo soldiers   The name Native Americans gave to African American cavalrymen, most of them Civil War veterans stationed in the West to fight the Indian wars of the 1870s and 1880s.

buying on the margin   The practice of buying stock or securities with a small down payment while financing the rest with borrowed money. When stock prices started to fall in 1929, brokers requested repayment of the loans. The funds were often not forthcoming, contributing to the crash of the stock market in October of that year.

C

cabinet The president's closest policy advisors. The first Congress organized bureaucratic departments to carry out the work of the executive branch. When elected president in 1789, George Washington (1789–1797) appointed secretaries of his choosing to run those departments. These secretaries, with whom he met on a regular basis, made up the president's cabinet.

Calvinism A religious doctrine of which the primary tenet is that a person's salvation is predestined by God. Founded by John Calvin of Geneva, Switzerland, during the Protestant Reformation, Calvinism required its adherents to live according to a strict religious and moral code. The Puritans who settled in colonial New England were devout Calvinists.

camp meetings *See* Second Great Awakening.

capital Wealth that is used to make more wealth. Capital is not spent on consumption or used up in the production of goods but rather generates more wealth that in turn can be used as capital. The self-perpetuating nature of capital allows for economic growth within a capitalist system, which explains the incredible growth of the U.S. economy after 1850.

capital goods Products such as machinery used by manufacturers to add to the productive capacity of the economy. In the late nineteenth century, the dramatic increase in capital goods used by businesses drove industrial expansion.

capitalism An economic system in which private individuals and corporations own and operate most means of production. Free-market competition—in which supply and demand is minimally regulated by the state or not regulated at all—determines the prices of goods and services. There are three major aspects of capitalism. First, a capitalist system generally includes many workers who do not own what they produce, but instead perform labor for wages. Second, capitalist societies move beyond local trade to the specialized production of goods for large-scale cash markets. Third, people in a capitalist society internalize a social mentality that emphasizes rationality and the pursuit of profit as the primary goal of economic life. In the United States, most regions made the transition to capitalism by the early nineteenth century. Over the following two hundred years, the United

States developed an industrial capitalist system, based on new technologies that allowed for self-sustaining economic growth.

caravel A type of small, agile sailing ship that became common in Spain and Portugal in the fifteenth century. Caravels allowed the Spanish and Portuguese to explore distant continents, including North and South America.

carpetbaggers A derisive name given by Southerners to Northerners who moved to the South during Reconstruction to help develop the region's economic potential and stabilize regional politics. Carpetbaggers included former soldiers and educated professionals. Former Confederates despised these Northern newcomers and saw them as exploiters. Though carpetbaggers played an important role in the Republican governments that held power in the South during radical Reconstruction, native Southerners regained control of their states in the 1870s. *See also* Reconstruction.

Catholicism The religion professed by members of the Roman Catholic Church. The Catholic Church has a hierarchical structure that places the pope at the head of the church. It emphasizes obedience to church superiors and absolution from sin through confession. Most of the first European immigrants to the New World were Protestants who believed the pope to be an unnecessary intermediary between God and His chosen; these believers demonized Catholics as papist enemies. In the nineteenth century, Irish and southern European Catholic immigrants faced social and economic discrimination. *See also* Protestantism.

caucus An informal meeting of politicians held by political parties to make majority decisions and enforce party discipline. Traditionally, members of Congress meet in party caucuses to select congressional leaders. Another style of caucus, called a participatory caucus, occurs in the United States in presidential election years. A participatory caucus, the best known of which is held in Iowa, may be attended by any eligible voter willing to acknowledge association with the party that holds it. In the early history of America, small groups of party leaders chose candidates for office in meetings called party caucuses. Since the 1830s, the major political parties have switched to using a national convention to nominate their candidates.

charter The right to form a local government, given to colonists by the English monarch. Charters legitimized English settlement in North America.

checks and balances A political system in which the executive, legislative, and judicial branches of the government curb each other's power. Checks and balances were written into the U.S. Constitution during the Constitutional Convention of 1787.

Chesapeake The English colonies (and later states) of Maryland and Virginia, on the Chesapeake Bay.

chivalry A code of behavior that emphasizes personal honor and male protection of female dependents. Chivalry was an important part of southern culture before the Civil War (1861–1865).

Church of England (Anglican Church) Protestant church created by Henry VIII in 1534 to supplant the Roman Catholic Church. Henry found himself at odds with both Catholics, who wanted to return the Church of England to the pope, and Protestants (Puritans), who wanted to further reform the church. After much waxing and waning under Henry's successors, Protestantism won out in England—but never to the Puritans' liking. Many Puritans departed for America in the seventeenth and eighteenth centuries to found communities devoted to their religious ideals. The mainstream Church of England also took root in America, particularly in the southern colonies. It separated from the Church of England following the Revolutionary War (1775–1783) and changed its name to the Episcopal Church. *See also* Catholicism.

Church of Jesus Christ of Latter-Day Saints *See* Mormonism.

"city on a hill" Biblical phrase from the New Testament used by Puritan leader John Winthrop in 1630 to articulate his vision for the Puritans' Massachusetts settlement. Winthrop wanted the emigrants to found an exemplary Christian community—a "city on a hill"—that would serve as a beacon for the Church of England, which they sought to reform from within.

civic humanism A concept that stressed service to the state and government to promote the good of the community. During the European Renaissance of the fifteenth and sixteenth centuries, a period of renewed interest in learning and the arts, this idea of selfless service was thought to be critical in a republic where control was vested in a politically active and committed citizenry. The concept was popular among the Founding Fathers and was an important ideology underlying the American constitutional government.

civil service The administrative service of a government. This term often applies to reforms following passage of the Pendleton Act in 1883, which set qualifications for U.S. government jobs and sought to remove such jobs from political influence.

clan A group of related families who share a common ancestor. In the sixteenth century, many native peoples north of the Rio Grande organized their societies around these groups, which often combined to form tribes.

clear and present danger test A standard established in the 1919 Supreme Court case *Schenck v. United States* to determine when the government could limit the right to free speech. *See also Schenck v. United States.*

closed shop A workplace in which every employee is required to join a union. In the late nineteenth century, craft unions began using closed shops to keep out incompetent and lower-wage workers. The use of closed shops became a controversial issue between workers and employers in the late nineteenth and early twentieth centuries.

closed-shop agreement A labor agreement common in the early twentieth century, in which an employer agrees to hire only union members. Those who believed such agreements undermined the authority of management worked to overturn them in the courts. In 1947, under the Taft-Hartley Act, closed shops and closed-shop agreements were declared illegal, but they continue to exist in practice.

Clovis people Early Paleo-Indians who settled in North and Central America between 13,500 and 11,000 BP; generally considered the first inhabitants of the Americas, although some archaeologists believe they were preceded by an earlier group. This nomadic hunting culture was named for Clovis, New Mexico, where one of their spearheads was first excavated. *See also* Paleo-Indians.

coffin ships Ships that brought a huge influx of Irish immigrants to the United States in the mid-nineteenth century. Malnourished from the Irish potato famine and crowded into disease-ridden quarters, many Irish died on the journey to America. Those who survived formed a large part of the industrial working class.

cold war The antagonistic relationship that existed between the Soviet Union and the United States and other Western nations from 1947 to 1989. This war was said to be cold because the hostility stopped short of armed (hot) conflict, which was warded off by the strategy of nuclear deterrence. Journalist Walter Lippmann popularized the term, using it as the title of his book on international relations in 1947.

collective bargaining A process of negotiation between labor unions and employers, particularly followed by the American Federation of Labor (AFL) in the late nineteenth century. Led by Samuel Gompers, the AFL accepted the new industrial order but fought for a bigger share of the profits for workers.

collective security An association of independent nations that agrees to accept and implement decisions made by the group, including going to war in defense of one or more members. The United States resolutely avoided such alliances until after World War II (1939–1945), when it created the North Atlantic Treaty Organization in response to the threat posed by the Soviet Union.

colonization The conquest and settlement of a region by a country or society. Beginning in the fifteenth century, several European countries colonized areas across the world, often subjecting native peoples to repressive rule.

Columbian exchange The transatlantic exchange of goods, peoples, and ideas that began when Christopher Columbus arrived in the Caribbean, ending the age-old separation of the hemispheres.

Committee on Public Information (CPI) An organization set up by President Woodrow Wilson (1913–1921) during World War I to increase support for America's participation in the war. Headed by journalist George Creel, the CPI was a national propaganda machine that helped create a political climate intolerant of dissent.

common law Traditional body of English legal rules and procedures that protected the king's subjects against arbitrary acts by the government. The U.S. legal system developed from English common law. The one exception is Louisiana, which modeled its legal system on the French civil law system.

commonwealth A group of people banded together for the common good; the term can be used for a state, a country, or a group of states or countries. Nations that sign a treaty pledging political or economic support to one another, such as the United Kingdom and its former colonies Australia and Canada, may call themselves a commonwealth. The United States may be called a commonwealth. Kentucky, Pennsylvania, Massachusetts, and Virginia refer to themselves as commonwealths rather than states. Puerto Rico and the Northern Mariana Islands are U.S. commonwealths.

communism A system of government in which a single authoritarian party controls the economy through state owner-ship of production, claiming to be working toward the dissolu-tion of the state and the even distribution of economic goods among the people. Communists around the globe encouraged the spread of communism in other nations in hopes of spark-ing worldwide revolution. At its peak in the 1930s, the Commu-nist Party of the United States worked closely with labor unions and insisted that only workers' overthrow of the capitalist sys-tem could save those suffering under of the Great Depression. After World War II, the Communist power and aspirations of the Soviet Union were held to be a direct threat to U.S. democracy, prompting the cold war. *See also* Marxism.

commutation A fee exempting wealthy men from compul-sory military service in the Civil War (1861–1865). The $300 commutation allowed them to hire substitutes to serve in their places. In the North, Democrats and their immigrant supporters attacked the loophole for favoring the rich at their expense. In the South, poor southern yeomen complained that commuta-tion made it "a rich man's war and a poor man's fight."

companionate marriage The conception of marriage as the union of loving partners rather than a political or economic arrangement in which the man held all the power. Empowered by republican ideas, women in the nineteenth century pressed for legal equality in matrimony. Even though husbands retained significant power as patriarchs, they increasingly viewed their wives as life companions rather than as inferiors or dependents.

complex marriage A form of open (nonmonogamous) marriage practiced by the utopian Oneida community in the mid-nineteenth century. Many utopian movements during this period experimented with gender roles.

Confederate States of America (CSA) Those states that seceded from the United States in 1861 to form a new political entity, thus sparking the Civil War (1881–1865).

conglomerate The business structure created when firms in different industries are purchased and combined into a single large firm. One purpose of this process is to ensure an overall profit even if one part of the firm operates at a loss. The conglomerate became more common in the final three decades of the twentieth century; by the end of that century, conglomerates made up three-fourths of all business mergers. *See also* merger.

Congregationalism The system of church governance in which local congregations govern themselves. Most of New England's churches from the mid-1600s to the early 1800s were Congregationalist; American Puritans and Separatists favored Congregationalism over both the Church of England's Episcopal system (government by bishops) and other denominations' presbytery system (government by church elders.) By freeing the church of most hierarchy, Puritans and Separatists believed they could keep the church free from corruption. The Congregational system could not, however, protect churches from the influx of new doctrines such as Unitarianism and transcendentalism, which altered many New England churches in the nineteenth century.

Congress of Racial Equality (CORE) An interracial civil rights organization formed in 1942. Its goals included equal rights, quality education, and economic and political opportunities for African Americans. In 1947, CORE staged Freedom Rides to test the enforcement of desegregation in interstate transportation. In 1960, the organization again staged Freedom Rides with the assistance of a newer civil rights organization, the Student Nonviolent Coordinating Committee. As the civil rights movement progressed, CORE moved from an interracial organization with black nationalist leanings that favored integration as a means to achieve its goal to a black organization that favored community control. *See also* Freedom Rides, Student Coordinating Committee.

conquistadors Spanish for "conquerors"; veterans of the wars against the Muslims, they followed the first Spanish explorers to the Americas in the early sixteenth century. The Spanish crown offered conquistadors plunder, estates in the conquered territory, and titles in return for creating an empire.

Conscience Whigs Politicians who opposed the Mexican-American War (1846–1848) on moral grounds, arguing that the purpose of the war was to acquire more land for the expansion of slavery. They believed that more slave states would destroy yeoman freeholder society and put slaveholders in charge of the federal government.

conscientious objector A person who refuses to aid in an armed conflict because of personal beliefs. In the United States, conscientious objectors have at times faced prison sentences for refusing to serve in the military or pay taxes in times of war, particularly during World War I (1914–1918) and the Vietnam War (1957–1975).

conscription *See* draft.

conservation The process of protecting the natural environment for sustained use. President Theodore Roosevelt (1901–1909) was a staunch conservationist, creating national parks and wildlife preserves and encouraging the efficient use of natural resources. Conservationists only took issue with those businesses that would exploit or monopolize public land. Preservationists, in contrast, opposed human development of government reserve land and sought to preserve the wilderness in its natural state.

conservatism A political and social doctrine, stressing stability and adherence to tradition, dating back to Alexander Hamilton's belief in a strong central government resting on a solid banking foundation. Economic conservatives place a high premium on low taxes and minimal government interference in the economy; social conservatives champion military preparedness, family values, and religious morality. Conservatism today is often associated with the Republican Party. *See also* liberalism.

conspicuous consumption A term first popularized by the economist Thorstein Veblen in the late nineteenth century to describe excessive spending on material goods. Consumption as a way to increase social status has been a frequently criticized feature of U.S. society. *See also* consumer culture.

constitution A formal document that establishes the fundamental laws and governing institutions of a society. The U.S. Constitution, signed on September 17, 1787, sets forth the form of America's national government and defines the rights and liberties of the people. The document was created to give more cohesiveness to the nation's political system than the Articles of Confederation (1781) had previously provided and in the process gave more power to Congress.

consumer culture A society that places high value on and devotes substantial resources to the purchase and display of material goods. Elements of U.S. consumerism were evident in the nineteenth century but really took hold in the twentieth century with installment buying and advertising in the 1920s and again with the postwar prosperity of the 1950s.

containment The U.S. foreign policy developed after World War II (1939–1945) to hold in check the power and influence of the Soviet Union and other groups or nations espousing communism. The strategy was first fully articulated by diplomat George F. Kennan in 1946–1947.

contrabands Slaves who fled the plantations for protection behind Union lines during the Civil War (1861–1865). Former slaves were an important source of manpower for the Union effort.

convoy A group of ships or other vehicles traveling together to guard against danger. In the face of threatening submarine warfare during World War I (1914–1918), convoys of U.S. and British merchant and troop ships were escorted by armed naval vessels. Organization in convoys greatly reduced the number of ships lost to German submarines, known as U-boats.

(CORE) *See* Congress of Racial Equality.

corporate colony A colony created by the granting of the right to self-government by the English monarch. Connecticut and Rhode Island were the only corporate colonies in North America.

corporation A business organization that raises money by issuing interest-bearing bonds of stock certificates that represent shares in ownership. Corporate structures allow people to invest in large and potentially risky economic ventures while limiting their own personal liability. In the late nineteenth century, corporations of all sorts—especially railroads—raised large amounts of capital to finance expansion, a key factor in spurring U.S. economic development.

cost-plus provisions Agreement between business and government in which industries were guaranteed a profit no matter what the cost of war production turned out to be; designed to enlist U.S. industry in the World War II (1939–1945) effort.

cotton gin A machine for processing cotton, invented in 1793 by Eli Whitney. The cotton gin greatly increased the profitability of cotton cultivation in the American South, sparking the expansion of slavery.

counterculture A culture embracing values or lifestyles opposing those of the mainstream culture. In the United States during the late 1960s, many young people created a counterculture that opposed the conservative social norms of Middle America. Hippies, people who oppose and reject conventional standards of society and advocate extreme liberalism in their sociopolitical attitudes and lifestyles, became synonymous with 1960s countercultural youth.

counterinsurgency A military operation using specially trained forces to defend against guerrilla warfare. The U.S. military created the Green Berets in the early 1960s to fight this type of nontraditional warfare, characteristic of the conflict in the Vietnam War (1957–1975). *See also* guerrilla warfare.

covenant A politically or religiously based agreement or pact. The Pilgrims used this term in the Mayflower Compact to refer to the agreement among themselves to establish a law-abiding community in which all members would work together for the common good. Later, New England Puritans used this term to refer to the agreement they made with God and each other to live according to God's will as revealed through Scripture. Early New England settlers saw their occupation of new lands as a religious pilgrimage ordained by God.

covert interventions Secret undertakings by a country or an organization in pursuit of foreign policy goals. The Central Intelligence Agency, begun in the 1950s, has regularly undertaken covert interventions such as U.S. participation in the 1954 overthrow of the Guatemalan government and support for the Nicaraguan Contras (Spanish counterrevolutionaries) in the 1980s. Knowledge of these acts was kept from the American people and most members of Congress.

coverture An English common-law doctrine adopted by the United States that incorporated women's civil, political, and economic rights into those of their husbands, leaving wives with no individual rights of their own. State-specific limitations to coverture began in the mid-nineteenth century, but until the twentieth century, most U.S. women, along with their property and children, were largely under the legal control of their husbands.

CPI *See* Committee on Public Information.

creationism The belief that a Supreme Being created Earth and all its life. Most creationists are Christians who base their beliefs on the Bible's story of creation. Creationism is in opposition to the scientific belief that life on Earth formed in an evolutionary process, as put forth by English scientist Charles Darwin in the 1850s. In the early 1900s, public schools began teaching evolution in science classes. In the 1920s, creationists proposed laws in 20 states to ban the teaching of evolution. In 1925, Thomas Scopes was found guilty of violating a Tennessee state law for teaching evolution. The struggle over the proper theory to teach in public schools continues into the twenty-first century. *See also* Darwinism.

credibility gap   The wide discrepancy between what was actually happening in the Vietnam War (1957–1975) and what the U.S. public was being told. The credibility of the U.S. position was increasingly undermined as more factual details were made public.

Creole   A person of European heritage born in the West Indies or Spanish America; or a descendant of French or Spanish colonists of the southern United States. The term is also a reference to the Spanish and Portuguese ruling over Indian populations in Latin America. "Creole" also refers to the French dialect spoken by the people of southern Louisiana. The term is also used more loosely to describe people of mixed race in the colonial Atlantic world.

crop lien system   The credit system that emerged in the rural South after the Civil War (1861–1865) in which furnishing merchants assumed ownership (or lien) of a borrower's crops as collateral for loans of seed, tools, and fertilizer. Southern governments passed laws permitting lien in the late nineteenth century, and both black and white sharecroppers who needed credit were forced to give merchants a lien on their crops. These merchants often charged high rates of interest and required their clients to grow single cash crops, trapping sharecroppers in a cycle of debt and preventing economic diversification away from the increasingly unprofitable cotton-based agriculture. *See also* sharecropping.

CSA   *See* Confederate States of America.

cult of domesticity   The nineteenth-century belief that women's place was in the home, where they should create a haven for harried men who worked in the outside world. This ideal was made possible by the separation of the workplace and the home, a result of the industrial revolution, and was used to sentimentalize the home and women's role in it.

cyberspace The virtual computer world that allows people across the globe to communicate with each other through the Internet. The term originated from William Gibson's 1984 novel *Neuromancer.* Since the 1980s, the meaning of the term has expanded from computer data floating around in the one computer's system or a small network of computers to the whole interconnected world of the Internet.

D

Darwinism The belief that living things evolved from simple organisms into more diverse and complex organisms over time, first put forth by English scientist Charles Darwin in the 1850s. Most scientists today accept this theory of evolution, and Darwinism is commonly taught in public schools, although creationists, who believe a Supreme Being created Earth, contest this theory. *See also* creationism.

deficit spending High government spending based on the ideas of economist John Maynard Keynes, who proposed in the 1930s that governments should be prepared to go into debt to stimulate a stagnant economy. *See also* pump priming.

deflation A decline in the general level of prices in a country's economy. The United States experienced sharp deflation during the Great Depression of the 1930s.

deindustrialization A long period of decline in the industrial sector. This term often refers specifically to the decline of manufacturing and the growth of the service sector of the economy in post–World War II America. Deindustrialization occurred through the use of more efficient and automated production techniques, increased competition from foreign-made goods, and the use of cheap labor abroad by U.S. manufacturers.

deism A religious belief associated with the Age of Reason and the Enlightenment (1700s) in which a rational, "watchmaker" God does not intervene directly in people's lives. Deists such as Benjamin Franklin rejected the authority of the Bible and relied on people's "natural reason" to define a moral code.

democracy A system of government in which the people have the power to rule, either directly or indirectly through their elected representatives. Believing that direct democracy was dangerous, the framers of the Constitution created a government that gave direct voice to the people only in the House of Representatives and that placed a check on that voice in the Senate by offering unlimited six-year terms to senators, elected by the state legislatures to protect them from the whims of democratic majorities. The framers further curbed the perceived dangers of democracy by giving each of the three branches of government (legislative, executive, and judicial) the ability to check the power of the other two.

Democratic Party One of the two major political parties of the United States, the other being the Republican Party. Established in 1828 to back Andrew Jackson (1829–1837) for the presidency, the Democratic Party branched off of the Democratic-Republican Party. Party members advocated majority rule and equality among the people and opposed special privileges for business corporations and the elite. In the 1860 presidential election, divided over the issue of slavery, the party offered both a northern Democrat and a southern Democrat as candidates. Later in the nineteenth century, the party drew its strength from the conservative segregated South and other rural areas; in the twentieth century, the Democrats became the party of labor, minorities, and other groups seeking more power in U.S. society. The Democratic Party is now generally viewed as the more liberal of the two major parties. *See also* Republican Party, solid South.

Democratic republicanism *See* republicanism.

depreciation A decrease in the value of currency or other asset. Depreciation may occur if there is a loss of value or of purchasing power resulting from an increase in the level of domestic prices. The Continental currency depreciated steadily between 1777 and 1780, and the depreciation rate of U.S. currency has ebbed and flowed with various economic cycles.

desegregation The process of ending segregation, or the forced separation of races. In the United States, the end of slavery brought institutionalized discrimination against African Americans in work, education, housing, and public services, particularly in the South. Beginning with the military in the 1950s, the federal government mandated desegregation, but faced stiff resistance from many southern states. The process of desegregation was not complete until the 1970s, and even today some racial separation persists in U.S. society.

détente French for "loosening"; refers to the easing of tensions between the United States and the Soviet Union during the Nixon administration.

deterrence The linchpin of U.S. military strategy during the cold war that dictated that the United States would maintain a nuclear arsenal so substantial the Soviet Union would refrain from attacking the United States and its allies out of fear that the United States would retaliate with an assault of devastating proportions. The Soviets pursued a similar strategy.

disarmament The voluntary limiting of stockpiling and use of weapons, usually through agreements between countries. Following World War II (1939–1945), the United Nations tried to obtain an agreement limiting arms for all nations. In the 1970s, the United States and the Soviet Union began meeting to limit nuclear weapon proliferation. Since the late 1980s, improved relations between the two countries have resulted in a number of arms-control agreements. One such agreement is the Strategic Arms Reduction Treaty (START) signed by U.S. President George H. W. Bush (1988–1993) and Soviet President Mikhail Gorbachev in 1991.

discount rate The interest level charged by the Federal Reserve for money it loans to member banks. Since its establishment in 1913, the Federal Reserve has had a powerful influence on the U.S. economy, due in large part to its ability to manipulate the discount rate.

disenfranchisement The denial of a person's right to vote. Despite the fact that the Fifteenth Amendment extended voting rights to blacks across the nation in 1970, most African Americans living in the South were disenfranchised until civil rights legislation of the mid-twentieth century enforced their right to vote.

disestablishment The movement after the American Revolution (1775–1783) to formally dissolve ties between church and state. The First Amendment to the Constitution prohibited Congress from passing laws regarding religion, but some states still recognized an official state church and prevented followers of another religion—such as Jews—from holding public office. Disestablishment was supported both by highly educated deists and by fervent new sects such as the Baptists, who feared that the state would corrupt the church rather than the other way around. Although government institutions retained a strong Protestant character, the lack of official preference for one sect or another resulted in the vibrant growth of various religious denominations. *See also* separation of church and state.

division of labor The separation of tasks in a larger manufacturing process. Although designed to improve efficiency and productivity, division of labor also limits workers' control over the conditions of their labor. Division of labor was a vital component of the industrial revolution in the 1800s.

Dixiecrats Members of the short-lived States' Rights Party, which broke with the Democratic Party in 1948 over civil rights issues. In more recent years, the term has referred to southern members of the Democratic Party who often vote for Republican or third-party candidates because of disagreements over social issues.

documentary impulse   Desire to present real-life situations in such a way as to evoke an emotional response; creating a document such as a film or photograph intended to elicit an empathetic reaction from its audience. During the New Deal, the Works Progress Administration's art projects were influenced by documentary impulse.

dole   Expression referring to direct payment of relief to the needy during the Great Depression, suggesting that relief money was doled out without recipients' having to perform work.

dollar diplomacy   The U.S. government's diplomatic initiatives to protect and enhance America's expanding business interests abroad in the early twentieth century.

dollar-a-year men   Leading businessmen called to Washington to help organize war mobilization at the beginning of World War II (1939–1945). Many of them stayed on the payrolls of their corporations and volunteered their services to the administration, receiving the nominal sum of a dollar a year.

domino theory   The assumption underlying U.S. foreign policy from the early cold war through the Vietnam War (1957–1975) that if one country fell to communism, neighboring countries would also fall under Communist control.

don't ask, don't tell   A federal policy announced in 1993 by President Bill Clinton (1993–2001) regarding the controversial issue of homosexuality in the military. Under this policy, military officials are forbidden to ask members of the armed forces about their sexuality but are allowed to dismiss personnel who do not hide their gay or lesbian orientations.

Double V campaign   The phrase coined by a leading black newspaper during World War II (1939–1945) to express that blacks fought for both "victory over our enemies at home and victory over our enemies on the battlefields abroad." The National Association for the Advancement of Colored People (NAACP) officially endorsed this Double V campaign and called for the government to extend black Americans the same privileges enjoyed by everyone else. While the Double V campaign boosted NAACP membership, it met with only limited success against racial discrimination during wartime.

doves Peace advocates, particularly during the Vietnam War (1957–1975). *See also* hawks.

dower right A legal right originating in medieval Europe and carried to the American colonies that extended to a widow the use of one-third of the family's land and goods during her lifetime.

downsizing The deliberate laying off of permanent employees to cut company costs and raise profits. In the 1980s and 1990s, the downsizing trend spread from entry-level workers to middle management.

draft A system for selecting individuals for conscription, or compulsory military service. Americans were first drafted during the Civil War (1861–1865). In 1940, Congress passed the Selective Service Act, which established the Selective Service System (SSS) to administer the draft needed during World War II (1939–1945). Between 1948 and 1973, during peacetime and periods of conflict, the SSS filled vacancies in the military with draftees. In 1973, amidst the Vietnam War (1957–1975), the government ended the draft and began accepting only volunteers into the armed forces. In 1980, Congress passed legislation resuming the required registration of all men ages 18 through 25 with the Selective Service.

***Dred Scott* decision** *See Scott v. Sandford.*

due process The legal doctrine, enshrined in the Fifth and Fourteenth Amendments to the Constitution, mandating that the government uphold all of a person's legal rights when depriving him or her of life, liberty, or property. Interpretation of what constitutes due process has been extremely controversial in U.S. history.

duel A formalized fight between two men, common from the Middle Ages through the nineteenth century. Duels were predicated on the concept of honor; men were socialized to protect their reputation from insult, even at the price of death. This concept of honor was especially strong in the U.S. South before the Civil War (1861–1865). Politicians Aaron Burr and Alexander Hamilton participated in a famous duel in 1804 that resulted in Hamilton's death.

E

Enlightenment The European cultural movement that reached America during the mid-1700s and emphasized rational and scientific thinking over traditional religion and superstition. Followers of the Enlightenment believed that human beings had the capability to analyze and affect the natural world, that individuals had a right to govern themselves, and that societies could be changed not by God, but through educational advancement and purposeful action.

environmental movement Activist movement begun in the 1960s that was concerned with protecting the environment through activities such as conservation, pollution control measures, and public awareness campaigns. In response to the new environmental consciousness, the federal government staked out a broad role in environmental regulation in the 1960s and 1970s. Lyndon Johnson (1963–1969) became the first president to send Congress a special message on the environment, obtaining measures to control air and water pollution and to preserve the American landscape. Richard Nixon (1969–1974) in turn created the Environmental Protection Agency in 1970. While the environmentalist movement achieved cleaner air and water and a reduction in toxic waste, it won only limited public endorsement. Most Americans favored economic expansion, personal acquisition, and convenience over environmental protection.

Episcopalian *See* Church of England.

Equal Rights Amendment The failed constitutional amendment stating that "equality of rights" must not be denied "on account of sex" that was first put before Congress by feminists in 1923. Opponents argued that the amendment would invalidate laws that protected women and would make women subject to the military draft. The amendment gained little support upon its initial proposal but was proposed again in the early 1970s. It passed through Congress but was ratified by only thirty-five states (five of which rescinded their ratification), falling three states short of the number needed to pass. Ratification failed again in the early 1980s.

Ethiopian Regiment A Loyalist military unit that consisted of one thousand escaped slaves, organized by Virginia's royal governor in the 1770s. This action, coupled with the governor's proclamation offering freedom to any slave who joined the Loyalist cause, pushed Virginia slaveholders to support the patriot cause.

ethnic cleansing The practice of entering a populated area during a time of civil strife and killing or driving away a significant portion of the population based on their ethnicity. The term was first used by Serbs seeking to seize territory from Muslims and Croats in the former Yugoslav provinces of Croatia and Bosnia. The violence in the late 1980s and early 1990s attracted international attention, which prompted President Bill Clinton (1993–2001) to bring leaders of Serbia, Croatia, and Bosnia to the United States in 1995, where they drew up a peace treaty. As part of the peacekeeping process, President Clinton agreed to send 20,000 American troops to Bosnia.

evangelicalism The trend in Protestant Christianity stressing salvation through conversion, repentance of sin, and adherence to Scripture; it also stresses the importance of preaching over ritual. During the Second Great Awakening in the 1820s and 1830s, evangelicals worshipped at camp meetings and religious revivals led by exuberant preachers.

excess-profits tax A levy on corporate profits and wealthy individuals during World War I (1914–1918). The tax accounted for more than half of all federal taxes and was a new source of federal government revenue.

excise levies Taxes imposed on goods such as salt, beer, and distilled spirits in late-eighteenth-century Britain, in part to fund wars in the American colonies. These taxes passed on the cost of imperial management to the king's subjects.

Exodusters African Americans who migrated to Kansas in the spring of 1879 to escape from the post-Reconstruction violence of the South. By 1880, 40,000 blacks lived in Kansas. *See also* Reconstruction.

Expansionism The policy of seeking land and trade beyond a country's boundaries to expand and improve upon national resources and economy. In contrast to those who advocated isolationism or avoiding world conflicts and markets, expansionists encouraged U.S. businesses to establish themselves overseas to turn greater profits and claim a larger piece of the world economy. U.S. exports soared in the late eighteenth century in particular.

The accompanying ideology of expansionism was that the superior Anglo-Saxon race had a mission to "civilize" the foreigners and Native Americans they encountered in their growing empire. *See also* Anglo-Saxonism, manifest destiny, social Darwinism, westward expansion.

expatriate A person who leaves his or her native country to live elsewhere, often motivated by political or ideological reasons. The term most commonly refers to a group of American artists and writers living in Paris after World War I (1914–1918). *See also* Lost Generation.

F

faction A small political group or alliance organized around a single issue or person. Factions often become the basis for political parties. In the eighteenth century, many considered factions dangerous because they were thought to undermine the stability of a community or nation.

factory Manufacturing business first created in the late eighteenth century that concentrated all the aspects of production under one roof, reorganized production, and divided work into specialized tasks. Factories made production faster and more efficient, while narrowing the range of worker activities and skills.

Fair Deal The domestic policy agenda announced by President Harry S. Truman (1945–1953) in 1949. His Fair Deal, named to underscore similarities with the New Deal of Franklin D. Roosevelt (1933–1945), included civil rights, health care, and education reform. Truman's initiative was only partially successful in Congress and was soon sidelined by foreign policy concerns. *See also* New Deal.

fascism An authoritarian system of government characterized by dictatorial rule, disdain for international stability, and a conviction that warfare is the only means by which a nation can attain greatness. The United States went to war against fascism when it faced Nazi Germany under Adolf Hitler and Italy under Benito Mussolini during World War II (1939–1945).

federal budget deficit The situation resulting when the government spends more money than it takes in. The U.S. government operated on a budget deficit from 1969 until 1998, when President Bill Clinton (1993–2001) recorded a budget surplus, meaning the government brought in more money than it spent.

Federal Reserve The central bank of the United States. The Federal Reserve controls the money supply, influences the rate of growth of the U.S. economy, and ensures the stability of the U.S. monetary system. *See also* money supply.

federalism A political system in which power is divided between a central government and smaller governmental units. The United States is a federal system. The Constitution defines the division of power between the central federal government and the smaller state units.

Federalist Party   One of the first political parties in the United States. The Federalist Party grew out of a fundamental disagreement at the Constitutional Convention as to how to structure the new country's government. The Federalists advocated a strong national government, arguing that a large polity checked by a balance of powers would best protect against the tyranny of a minority over the interests of the majority. Their opponents, the Antifederalists, feared that a centralized government would erode local political participation and encourage corruption. The Federalist plan prevailed and was enshrined in the Constitution. In the late eighteenth and early nineteenth centuries, the Federalists advocated conservative policies aimed at stimulating economic growth and consolidating elite power, such as the establishment of a national bank, protective tariffs, friendship with Britain, and condemnation of the radical egalitarianism of the French Revolution. *See also* Antifederalists.

fee simple   The legal status of English land titles in seventeenth-century Puritan society. Landowners who held fee simple titles possessed their land outright, free from manorial obligations or feudal dues.

Feminine Mystique, The   The title of an influential book written in 1963 by Betty Friedan critiquing the ideal whereby women were encouraged to confine themselves to roles within the domestic sphere. The feminist movements during the years emerged in reaction to this ideology of separate spheres.

feminism   The belief that women have the identical inherent right to equal social, political, and economic opportunities as men. The suffrage movement of the nineteenth and early twentieth centuries and the women's rights movement of the 1960s and 1970s (often called second-wave feminism) were the most visible and successful manifestations of feminism, but feminist ideas were expressed in a variety of statements and movements as early as the late eighteenth century. Beginning in the 1990s, responding to an antifeminist backlash, young women spearheaded a "third wave" of feminism, considering issues of race, class, ethnicity, sexual orientation, and age alongside gender issues. Feminists continue today to influence social, political, and economic spheres in the United States.

filibuster   A strategy used in the U.S. Senate to prevent legislation from coming to a vote. During a filibuster, senators employ delaying tactics, usually long speeches, to force abandonment of an issue. In 2005, the Senate considered a proposal to ban the use of filibusters when considering judicial nominees for the Supreme Court.

fire-eaters Southern proslavery extremists who sought secession from the Union. Fire-eaters organized secession conventions in several southern states in 1850 but backed down because of a lack of support and the promise of moderate southern backing for secession if Congress tried to outlaw slavery in the future. *See also* secession.

fireside chat President D. Franklin Roosevelt's (1933–1945) regularly scheduled radio broadcasts to the public in the 1930s and 1940s. The name suggested an intimate conversation and demonstrated the president's effective use of the new electronic political medium of radio.

First Great Awakening *See* Great Awakening.

flapper A young woman of the 1920s who defied conventional standards of conduct by wearing short skirts and makeup, freely spending the money she earned on the latest fashions, dancing to jazz, and flaunting her liberated lifestyle. The flapper was a cultural icon of the era, but actually represented only a small minority of women.

flexible response Military strategy employed by the John F. Kennedy (1961–1963) and Lyndon B. Johnson (1963–1969) administrations. This strategy was designed to match a wide range of military threats by complementing nuclear weapons with the buildup of conventional and special forces and employing them all in a gradual and calibrated way as needed. Flexible response was a departure from the strategy of massive retaliation used by the Dwight D. Eisenhower (1953–1961) administration.

forty-niners The more than 80,000 settlers who descended on California in 1849 as part of that territory's gold rush. Forty-niners are one example of the American tendency to take risks and travel long distances in search of prosperity. *See also* gold rush.

Four Freedoms Used by President Franklin D. Roosevelt (1933–1945) to describe the most basic human rights: freedom of speech, freedom of religion, freedom from want, and freedom from fear. The president used these ideas of freedom to justify support for England during World War II (1939–1945), which in turn pulled the United States into the war. *See also* human rights.

Fourierism A movement based on the ideas of Charles Fourier, a French social theorist who advocated cooperation, not competition. Fourierist communities, called phalanxes, sprang up in the northern United States in the 1840s. *See also* phalanx.

Fourteen Points Principles for a new world order proposed in 1919 by President Woodrow Wilson (1913–1921) as a basis for peace negotiations at Versailles. Among them were open diplomacy, freedom of the seas, free trade, territorial integrity, arms reduction, national self-determination, and the League of Nations. *See also* League of Nations.

franchise The right to vote. The franchise was gradually widened in the United States to include groups such as blacks and women, who had no vote in federal elections when the Constitution was ratified. In 1971, the Twenty-Sixth Amendment lowered the voting age from twenty-one to eighteen.

free labor Work conducted free from constraint and in accordance with the laborer's personal inclinations and will. Prior to the Civil War (1861–1865), the free labor system became an ideal championed by Republicans (who were primarily northerners) to articulate individuals' right to work how and where they wished and to accumulate property in their own names. The ideal of free labor lay at the heart of the North's argument that slavery should not be extended into the western territories.

free market *See* laissez-faire.

free silver The late-nineteenth-century call by silver barons and poor U.S. farmers for the widespread coinage of silver and for silver to be used as a base upon which to expand the paper money supply. The coinage of silver created an inflationary monetary system that benefited debtors. *See also* gold standard.

free soil The idea advanced in the 1840s that Congress should prohibit slavery within western territories because it threatened republican institutions and yeoman farming. "Free soil, free speech, free labor, and free men" became the rallying cry of the short-lived Free-Soil Party.

freedom of religion One of the fundamental rights enshrined in the First Amendment to the Constitution, prohibiting government favoritism of some religions over others and affirming the right of individual Americans to practice any faith they choose.

freedom of speech One of the fundamental rights enshrined in the First Amendment to the Constitution, affirming the right of Americans to voice and disseminate their views without penalty.

Freedom Rides A form of civil rights protest for which the Congress of Racial Equality organized racially mixed groups to travel by bus throughout the South in 1961 to test compliance with federal laws banning racial segregation on interstate transportation. These activists were subjected to violence in several southern cities and drew the John F. Kennedy (1961–1963) administration further into the struggle for equal rights.

freehold Ownership of a plot of land and possession of the title or deed. Freeholders have the legal right to improve, transfer, or sell their property. This type of landholding characterized New England in the seventeenth and eighteenth centuries, as its founders attempted to avoid the concentration of land in the hands of an elite—an undesirable characteristic of the England that they had left.

frontier A borderland area. In U.S. history, this refers to the borderland between the areas primarily inhabited by Europeans or their descendants and the areas solely inhabited by Native Americans. Inhabitants of the eastern areas of North America ventured further west as the East grew more populous, seeking land and prosperity. *See also* westward expansion.

fugitive slave A runaway slave before the Civil War (1861–1865). Runaway slaves were declared fugitives by their former owners, and the Fugitive Slave Act of 1850 required northern states to return escapees to their owners.

fundamentalism Strict adherence to core, often religious, beliefs. The term has varying meanings for different religious groups. Protestant fundamentalists adhere to a literal interpretation of the Bible and thus deny the possibility of evolution. Muslim fundamentalists believe that traditional Islamic law should govern nations and that Western influences should be banned.

G

gag rule A procedure in the House of Representatives from 1836 to 1844 by which antislavery petitions were automatically tabled when they were received so that they could not become the subject of debate.

GDP *See* gross domestic product.

gender gap An electoral phenomenon that became apparent in the 1980s when men and women began to display different preferences in voting. Women tended to favor liberal candidates, and men tended to support conservatives. The key voter groups contributing to the gender gap were single women (with and without children) and women who worked outside the home.

ghetto An urban neighborhood composed of the poor; occasionally the word used to describe any tight-knit community containing a single ethnic or class group. Ghettos came into being in the nineteenth century, in tandem with the enormous influx of immigrants to U.S. cities.

Ghost Dance A religious movement that swept the Plains Indians in 1890. It stemmed from the preaching of the Paiute prophet Wovoka, who claimed that the whites would disappear from the Great Plains and that Indians would reclaim their lands.

GI Bill Popular name for the Servicemen's Readjustment Act of 1944, which sought to ease the transition of World War II (1939–1945) veterans back into civil society. The GI Bill supplied veterans with job training, education, unemployment compensation, and low-interest loans, resulting in upward mobility for many thousands of U.S. families.

Gibson girl The image of the "new woman" created during the 1890s by illustrator Charles Dana Gibson. The Gibson girl represented a stronger, more independent vision of women as well as a more sexual one.

Gilded Age A period of enormous economic growth and ostentatious displays of wealth during the last quarter of the nineteenth century. The social and economic reorganization brought about by the industrial revolution resulted in dramatic changes in U.S. society, including a newly dominant group of rich entrepreneurs and an impoverished working class. *See also* industrialization.

glasnost The policy introduced by Soviet president Mikhail Gorbachev during the 1980s that referred to greater openness and freedom of expression. Gorbachev's policies during his presidency contributed to the freeing of Eastern Europe from Soviet domination and led, unintentionally, to the 1991 breakup of the Soviet Union. *See also perestroika.*

globalization The spread of political, cultural, and economic influences and connections among countries, businesses, and individuals around the world through trade, immigration, communication, and other means. In the late twentieth century, globalization was intensified by new communications technology that connected individuals, corporations, and nations with greater speed at lower prices. This led to an increase in political and economic interdependence and mutual influence among nations.

GDP *See* gross national product.

gold rush An influx of fortune seekers into an area following rumors of extractable gold. In the United States, the largest gold rushes occurred in the mid-nineteenth century in California and in the late nineteenth century in Alaska. In California, the rapid population increase propelled the region toward statehood, heightening national tensions over slavery.

gold standard A monetary system in which circulating currency is exchangeable for a specific amount of gold. Advocates for the gold standard believe that gold alone should be used for coinage and that the total value of paper banknotes should never exceed the government's supply of gold. The triumph of gold standard advocate William McKinley in the 1896 presidential election was a big victory for supporters of this policy.

gospel of wealth The idea that wealth garnered from earthly success should be used for good works. Steel manufacturer and millionaire Andrew Carnegie promoted this view in an 1889 essay in which he maintained that the wealthy should serve as stewards and act in the best interests of society as a whole. Gilded Age financiers supplied the funds for many enduring public institutions. *See also* Gilded Age.

government bonds Promissory notes issued by a government to borrow money from members of the public. Such bonds are redeemable at a set future date, and bondholders earn interest on their investment. People were particularly encouraged to buy bonds during World War II (1939–1945) as part of the home-front effort.

Great American Desert   The name given to the drought-stricken Great Plains by Euro-Americans in the early nineteenth century. Believing the region was unfit for cultivation or agriculture, Congress designated the Great Plains as permanent Indian country in 1834.

Great Awakening   The widespread movement of religious revitalization in the 1730s and 1740s that emphasized vital religious faith and personal choice. It was characterized by large, open-air meetings at which emotional sermons were given by itinerant preachers. This movement is sometimes referred to as the First Great Awakening, to differentiate it from a later movement in the 1820s and 1830s, known as the Second Great Awakening.

Great Depression   The severe, worldwide economic downturn following the crash of the U.S. stock market in 1929. Causes of the depression included speculation, reckless financial practices, and a serious imbalance of supply and demand that had resulted in overproduction. Over the next decade, global suffering intensified as economic activity ground virtually to a halt. The U.S. economy did not fully recover until World War II (1939–1945) reinvigorated industry.

great migration   The migration of over 400,000 African Americans from the rural South to the industrial cities of the North during and after World War I (1914–1918). Employment opportunities created by the war gave rise to a new class of urban African Americans, many of whom thrived in the freer northern environment.

Great Society   President Lyndon B. Johnson's (1963–1969) domestic program, which included civil rights legislation, anti-poverty programs, government subsidy of medical care, federal aid to education, consumer protection, and aid to the arts and humanities. Great Society programs enjoyed some success but were ultimately limited by conflicting interest groups, political infighting, and lack of funds.

Great War   Popular name for World War I (1914–1918), which saw new and powerful weapons, incredible bloodshed, and dramatic political changes in Europe.

greenbacks Any paper currency issued by the federal government as legal tender. Greenbacks were first issued by the Union during the Civil War (1861–1865) to finance the war effort. The value of greenbacks is backed by the good faith of the government rather than by gold or silver.

gross domestic product (GDP) A measure of economic production. GDP is the value of all the goods and services produced within a country during a year, regardless of the nationality of the owners of those goods and services.

gross national product (GNP) A measure of economic production. GNP is the value of all the goods and services produced by a country's citizens, regardless of where production takes place.

guerrilla warfare Fighting carried out by an irregular military force usually organized into small, highly mobile groups. Guerrilla combat was common during the Revolutionary War (1775–1783), when colonists adapted Native American combat techniques to fight the highly regimented British troops, and during the Vietnam War (1957–1975). Guerrilla warfare is often effective against opponents who have greater material resources.

H

habeas corpus The constitutional right that protects citizens against arbitrary arrest and detention. During the Civil War (1861–1865), President Abraham Lincoln (1861–1865) suspended *habeas corpus* to stop protests against the draft and other disloyal activities. Lincoln also transferred cases of disloyalty from civilian to military jurisdiction, fearing that local juries would treat Confederate sympathizers leniently.

Halfway Covenant A Puritan compromise that allowed the unconverted children of the "visible saints" (God's chosen ones) to become halfway members of the church. The Halfway Covenant allowed these halfway members to baptize their own children even though they themselves were not full members of the church because they had not experienced full conversion. Massachusetts ministers accepted this compromise in 1662, marking a shift in the religious character of New England society.

hard currency Money coined directly from, or backed in full by, precious metals (particularly gold). Also known as hard money. *See also* gold standard, specie.

Harlem Renaissance The group of African American artists, intellectuals, and social leaders who lived in Harlem in the 1920s. They were termed the New Negroes by black professor Alain Locke because they had risen from the ashes of slavery to proclaim African American creative genius and work toward defeating racial prejudice.

hawks Advocates of aggressive military action or all-out war, particularly during the Vietnam War (1957–1975). *See also* doves.

headright A program begun by the Virginia Company in 1617 that granted the head of a household fifty acres for himself and fifty additional acres for every adult family member or servant brought into the Virginia colony.

hegemony Dominance in global affairs by a nation. The United States and the Soviet Union emerged from World War II (1939–1945) as the world's leading powers, each exercising a tremendous influence within their respective spheres of influence.

heresy A religious doctrine inconsistent with the teaching of an established, official Christian church. In seventeenth-century New England, those who practiced traditional folk medicine, claimed to have visions, or otherwise expressed beliefs that contradicted those of Puritanism were vulnerable to accusations of heresy. Puritan Anne Hutchinson was exiled from the Massachusetts Bay Colony for the heresy of prophesy—that God was speaking to her directly rather than through the Bible. Charles Darwin, who promoted the theory of evolution, was called a heretic by those who believed that God created the Earth.

Hessians German soldiers hired by the British to fight during the Revolutionary War (1775–1783). About 30,000 Hessians fought against the American colonists.

hippie A young person who participated in the 1960s counterculture, a lifestyle in which drug use, rock music, uninhibited sexuality, and vivid self-expression were celebrated. *See also* counterculture.

holding company A system of business organization whereby competing companies are combined under one central administration to curb competition and ensure profit. Pioneered in the late 1880s by Standard Oil Company founder John D. Rockefeller, holding companies exercised monopoly control even as the government threatened to outlaw trusts as a violation of free trade. *See also* monopoly, trust.

home rule The ideal of white supremacist rule without federal interference championed by southern Democrats hoping to overthrow legitimately elected Reconstruction governments after the Civil War (1861–1865). By 1876, both national parties, Republican and Democrat, favored home rule. *See also* Reconstruction.

homespun Yarn and cloth produced by American women. During political boycotts in the 1760s, homespun allowed the colonies to escape dependence on British textile manufactures and created an opportunity for women to make a unique contribution to the colonial resistance.

homestead A residence or piece of land, usually a farm. The Homestead Act of 1862 gave 160 acres of free western land to any person willing to settle on it for at least five years. This policy led to the rapid development of the American West after the Civil War (1861–1865).

honest graft The financial advantages of insider information in the awarding of city contracts, indicating one aspect of urban machine politics.

horizontal integration The acquisition of a number of businesses selling a similar product to gain additional strength in that market. In the late nineteenth century, John D. Rockefeller's Standard Oil Company purchased forty oil refineries, giving it a virtual monopoly over the oil refinery business. Rockefeller then began to employ the vertical integration strategy of steel producer Andrew Carnegie, becoming involved in other parts of the oil production process. *See also* vertical integration.

House Un-American Activities Committee (HUAC) The committee created to investigate alleged Communist infiltration of government agencies and other institutions. HUAC famously investigated hundreds of people in the film industry in 1947 as part of a general anti-Communist hysteria. Such tactics imposed a climate of fear and quelled political debate in the United States during the late 1940s and early 1950s. *See also* communism, McCarthyism.

household mode of production The system of exchanging goods and labor that helped eighteenth-century New England freeholders survive on ever-shrinking farms as available land became more scarce.

HUAC *See* House Un-American Activities Committee.

human rights Fundamental, universal rights held by all people. Although most countries agree that human rights do exist, there is some debate over the specific definition of those rights. The United Nations Universal Declaration of Human Rights, adopted in 1948, includes rights to life, self-determination, and education, as well as freedom of expression and movement.

I

ICBMs *See* intercontinental ballistic missiles.

impeachment The process by which formal charges of wrongdoing are brought against a president, a governor, or a federal judge. Impeachment can result in the removal of an official from office. The House of Representatives has the sole power to impeach. Upon the issue of the articles of impeachment by the House, the Senate sits as a court to hear the charges. The House of Representatives has voted articles of impeachment only sixteen times, twelve of which were against judges. The Senate has convicted only seven people, all of whom were judges. Only two presidents, Andrew Johnson (1965–1869) and Bill Clinton (1993–2001), have been impeached; neither president was convicted. President Richard Nixon (1969–1974) resigned before the House voted on articles of impeachment recommended against him by the House Judiciary Committee.

imperial presidency The growth of executive power, based on attempts by President Richard Nixon (1969–1974) in 1972 to subvert the constitutional restraints on his authority.

imperialism The system by which great powers gain control of overseas territories. The late 1800s is often called the Age of Imperialism. The United States became an imperialist power by gaining control of Puerto Rico, Guam, the Philippines, and Cuba as a result of the Spanish-American War (1898).

import substitution The government policy of encouraging the growth of domestic industry, usually through subsidies and high tariffs. *See also* tariff.

impoundment The refusal of a president to spend money appropriated by Congress. In the early 1970s, President Richard Nixon (1969–1974) hoped to slow the growth of the federal government and reduce funding for programs he opposed by refusing to spend money appropriated by the Democratic-controlled Congress for urban renewal and pollution control.

impressment Forcible, unwilling draft into military service. The British navy forced American merchant sailors into service in the years preceding the War of 1812 (1812–1814), greatly increasing tensions between the two nations.

indentured servitude A system that committed poor immigrants to between four and seven years of labor in exchange for passage to the American colonies and food and shelter after they arrived. An indenture is a type of contract. Indentured servants were the primary source of labor in the American colonies in the early years of settlement.

Indian removal The process of forcibly removing Indians from desirable lands and relocating them west of the Mississippi River in the early nineteenth century. Indian removal was carried out largely under the leadership of President Andrew Jackson (1829–1837).

Indian schools Schools set up in the late nineteenth century to "civilize" Indian children and assimilate them into white society. Although some of these boarding schools were supervised by the tribes themselves, others were filled with children who had been forcibly removed from their homes.

individualism Coined by Alexis de Tocqueville in 1835 to describe Americans as people no longer bound by social attachments to classes, castes, associations, and families. Some observers worried that individualism was a cause of social disorder; others saw it as liberating.

industrial revolution The period during the late 1700s and early 1800s when industrialization caused tremendous changes in the lives and work of people in a number of regions in the Western world. The industrial revolution began in Britain; by the mid-1800s, industrialization was widespread in western Europe and the northeastern United States. *See* industrialization.

industrial union A group of workers in a single industry (for example, automobile, railroad, or mining) organized into a single association, regardless of skill, rather than into separate craft-based associations. The American Railway Union, formed in the 1880s, was one of the first industrial unions in the nation.

industrialization The transition of an economy to self-sustaining growth, largely through technological advances and the reorganization of labor. In the late eighteenth and early nineteenth centuries, England was the first country to make this transition. By the early twentieth century, the United States, with its vast natural resources and diverse regional markets, became the world's foremost industrial power. *See also* industrial revolution.

inflation A continual increase in prices throughout a country's economy. Inflation often occurs in the years following a war, when the supply of goods is low and consumer demand is high. In 1919, after World War I (1914–1918), prices rose 75 percent above prewar prices.

influenza A highly contagious respiratory disease, also known as the grippe or the flu. In 1918 and 1919, a particularly severe form of influenza, sometimes called Spanish influenza after a large outbreak in Spain, killed millions worldwide. More U.S. soldiers in World War I (1914–1918) died of influenza than of war-related injuries.

inmates A new class of the poor in the eighteenth century, made up of Scots-Irish single men or families who possessed little property and existed as tenants or day laborers with little hope of earning economic independence.

integration The process of ending racial segregation in the United States, particularly in the American South, in the 1950s and 1960s. Supporters of civil rights pushed for the integration of schools and other public and private institutions, ending the discriminatory "separate but equal" system. *See* "separate but equal" doctrine.

intercontinental ballistic missiles (ICBMs) Nuclear missiles capable of traveling more than 5,000 kilometers, first produced in the United States in the 1950s. After the Soviet Union developed its own ICBMs in 1957, the most intense arms race in history ensued. *See also* cold war.

interest rate A percentage of the value of a loan paid by a borrower to a lender in return for the loan. The banking interest rates set by the Federal Reserve, the central bank of the United States, influence economic growth by encouraging or discouraging investments.

Internet A vast network of communication technology made possible by the computer revolution and supporting tools such as e-mail and the World Wide Web that became increasingly popular in the 1990s.

interstate slave trade Slave trade between states that continued after the abolition of the Atlantic slave trade in 1808. Slaves were most often sold from the Upper South to the Lower South, a move undesirable to slaves because it usually meant harder labor and less chance of escape. The interstate slave trade broke up many slave families in the decades preceding the Civil War (1861–1865).

iron curtain A metaphor coined by British prime minister Winston Churchill during his commencement address at Westminster College in Fulton, Missouri, in 1946. Churchill used *iron curtain* to refer to the political, ideological, and military barriers that separated Soviet-controlled Eastern Europe from the rest of Europe and the West following World War II (1939–1945).

isolationism A U.S. foreign policy perspective characterized by a desire to withdraw from world conflicts and enjoy the protection of two vast oceans. During much of the nineteenth century and the period between the two World Wars (1918–1939), the United States favored a policy of isolationism. Since the end of World War II (1945), the U.S. government has been able to convince the majority of the U.S. public that they should abandon isolationism and act as a great world power.

J

Jazz Age Another name for the 1920s, or the Roaring Twenties. The period was marked by rapid economic growth, rising prosperity for many people, and far-reaching social changes for much of the nation. Jazz, a new genre of music developed by creole musicians in New Orleans, became increasingly popular during the period, and the style became synonymous with the decade.

Jim Crow The system of racial segregation that developed in the post–Civil War South and extended well into the twentieth century; it replaced slavery as the chief instrument of white supremacy. Jim Crow laws segregated African Americans in public facilities such as trains and streetcars and denied them basic civil rights, including the right to vote. During this time period, the doctrine of "separate but equal" became institutionalized. *See Plessy v. Ferguson,* segregation.

jingoism Extreme nationalism marked by belligerent foreign policy, an attitude held by many late-nineteenth-century Americans. Proponents of this approach are called jingoes. Jingoism was epitomized by President Theodore Roosevelt (1901–1909), who believed that nations and individuals needed warfare to maintain their virility.

joint-stock company A financial arrangement established by the British to facilitate the colonization of the New World in the seventeenth century. Joint-stock agreements allowed merchants to band together as stockholders, raising large amounts of money while sharing the risks and profits in proportion to their part of the total investment.

Judaism The ancient monotheistic religion that formed the basis for and shared many of its ethical principles with Christianity. Judaism is a decentralized religion that emphasizes action over belief. Although the United States was largely a Christian country during colonial times and the early Republic, small Jewish communities existed along the eastern seaboard and were happy to note that the Constitution did not name Christianity as the state religion. Facing harsh repression in Europe, Jews immigrated to the United States in large numbers at the end of the nineteenth and beginning of the twentieth centuries. The passage of the Johnson-Reid Act in 1924, which severely restricted the number of immigrants allowed from Southern and Eastern European countries with large Catholic and Jewish populations, reflected the prevalence of anti-Semitism, or hostility toward Jews, among rural and Protestant Americans. This prejudice and an unwillingness to believe reports of Nazi concentration camps in Europe kept many Americans from supporting relaxed immigration quotas for Jewish refugees during World War II.

judicial review The right of the courts to judge the constitutionality of laws passed by Congress and the state legislatures. This power is implicit within the federal Constitution and was first practiced by the Supreme Court in *Marbury v. Madison* in 1803. *See also Marbury v. Madison.*

K

kamikaze Aerial Japanese suicide attacks during World War II (1939–1945) in which pilots crashed their planes into U.S. ships in a last-ditch effort to destroy the U.S. naval forces. This tactic became increasingly common as the war in the Pacific turned more desperate for Japan.

Keynesian economics A theory developed by English economist John Maynard Keynes that guided U.S. economic policy from the New Deal to the 1970s. According to Keynesians, the federal government has a duty to stimulate and manage the economy by spending money on public works projects and by making general tax cuts to put more money into the hands of ordinary people, thus creating more demand for goods. *See* New Deal, supply-side economics.

King Cotton Used to express the dominance of cotton in the economy of the antebellum South (1812–1860). The strong demand for cotton in industrial Britain enriched southern planters and determined the course of southern economic and social development.

KKK *See* Ku Klux Klan.

Know-Nothings A nativist political party that enjoyed a brief popularity in the decade before the Civil War (1861–1865). The Know-Nothings drew on anti-Catholic and anti-immigrant sentiment to gain power across the country in 1854 and 1855. Within a couple of years, however, sectionalism (regional loyalties) proved to be a more potent political force than nativism. *See also* nativism.

Ku Klux Klan (KKK) A white supremacist group that arose in the South after the Civil War (1861–1865). The Ku Klux Klan sought to intimidate the African American population through violence and murder, assaulting those who claimed political, economic, or social equality with whites. The government intervened in the 1870s, enacting the Ku Klux Klan Act in hopes of ending white terrorism, but the KKK was revived amidst anti-foreign sentiments in the 1920s. Klan members considered the influx of immigrants a threat to traditional American values and viewed themselves as defenders of white Protestant morality.

L

labor movement The efforts of workers as a group, often as a union, trying to improve their economic position and general welfare. The labor movement became increasingly accepted in the United States during the 1930s when the government passed a number of laws, including the National Labor Relations Act (1935), that required companies to bargain with unions. By 1945, more than a third of all nonagricultural laborers were union members. Organized labor is still powerful in the United States today.

labor theory of value The belief that the price of a product should reflect the work that went into making it and should be paid mostly to the person who produced it. This idea was popularized by the National Trades' Union in the mid-nineteenth century.

laissez-faire The doctrine, based on economic theory, that government should not interfere in business or the economy. Laissez-faire ideas guided U.S. government policies in the late nineteenth century and conservative politics in the twentieth. Business interests that supported laissez-faire in the late nineteenth century accepted government interference when it took the form of tariffs or subsidies that worked to their benefit. "Laissez-faire" is often used interchangeably with "free market" when referring to the economy. Broader uses of the term refer to the simple philosophy of abstaining from all government interference.

lame duck An elected official who is serving out his or her last term in office. The Twentieth Amendment to the Constitution, passed in 1933, provides that the president's term of office begins on January 20 (changed from March 4) and that the terms of congressional members begin on January 3. This lame-duck amendment was designed to limit the time an unseated public official continues to serve with diminished power.

land grant A gift of land from a government, usually intended to encourage settlement or development. The British government issued several land grants to encourage development in the American colonies. In the mid-nineteenth century, the U.S. government issued land grants to encourage railroad development and, through passage of the Land-Grant College Act (also known as the Morrill Act) in 1863, set aside public lands to support universities.

League of Nations The international organization bringing together world governments, proposed by President Woodrow Wilson (1913–1921) in the aftermath of World War I (1914–1918). The League of Nations sought to prevent future hostilities through diplomacy and cooperative action. Despite Wilson's support, the United States never became a member, and the League was replaced by the United Nations after World War II (1939–1945).

liberalism A political and social doctrine holding that government rests on the consent of the governed and is duty-bound to protect the freedom and property of the individual. Economic liberals believe that the government should regulate the economy and protect individual rights. Social liberals believe that the government should ensure the material well-being and general welfare of all people, and cultural liberals espouse multiculturalism and tolerance. Liberalism today is often associated with the Democratic Party. *See also* conservatism.

libertarianism A political ideology that believes in increasing individual liberties and limiting government activities. The Libertarian Party was founded in the United States in 1971. The party opposes government aid to and regulation of business. It favors neutral foreign policy, including withdrawal from the United Nations and limitation to or end of military action abroad.

liberty The condition of being free or enjoying freedom from control. This term also refers to the possession of certain social, political, or economic rights such as the right to own and control property. Eighteenth-century American colonists evoked the principle to argue for strict limitations on government's ability to tax its subjects.

lien *See* crop lien system.

limited liability Contractual clause ensuring that the personal assets of shareholders cannot be seized to cover the debts of a corporation. By 1800, state governments had granted more than three hundred corporate charters, many of which included limited liability clauses. Limited liability was a vital factor in the development of large-scale industry because it enabled companies to acquire large amounts of capital from a wide variety of investors who were previously unwilling to risk their entire personal fortunes in their investments.

living wage A wage sufficient to provide for the basic needs of a worker and all of his or her dependents, also sometimes called the family wage. The push for living wages strengthened considerably in the final decade of the twentieth century. In 1994, Baltimore became the first city to adopt a living wage ordinance.

Long Drive The moving of wild longhorn cattle hundreds of miles from Texas to the railheads of Kansas, where they could be shipped to eastern markets. This seemingly colorful event was actually a makeshift means of bridging a gap in the developing transportation system. The Long Drive was abandoned when the railroads reached the Texas range country during the 1870s.

los pobres Spanish for "the poor ones"; Hispanic residents of New Mexico who were displaced when Anglo ranchers fenced communal lands. These residents organized themselves as masked raiders and in 1889 and 1890 mounted an effective campaign of harassment against the interloping ranchers.

Lost Generation The phrase coined by writer Gertrude Stein to refer to the young artists and writers who felt alienated from America's mass-culture society in the 1920s. These individuals (including Ernest Hemingway, F. Scott Fitzgerald, Sinclair Lewis, and Stein herself) believed that business values blighted nearly every aspect of American life and loathed the adoration of popular culture celebrities such as movie stars. Embittered over the war and the progressives who promoted it, members of the Lost Generation left the United States for Europe, often settling in Paris, France, along with Stein. *See also* expatriates.

loyalist An American colonist who remained loyal to the British monarchy during the Revolutionary War (1775–1783). Loyalists, also called Tories, accounted for 20 to 30 percent of the American population (with another 20 to 40 percent remaining neutral). Colonists chose to stay loyal to the monarchy for a multitude of reasons. Many still felt strong cultural and economic ties to Britain and believed that American prosperity depended on British rule. Some feared democratic tyranny and the loss of hierarchy. Pockets of loyalists existed throughout the colonies, with royal officials represented in high numbers. After the British defeat, a sizable number of loyalists returned to England for fear of reprisal.

lynching Extralegal executions typically performed by mobs against marginalized groups. Lynchings of black men were especially common in the South during the decades between the end of the Civil War (1861–1865) and the civil rights movement. Between 1889 and 1910, 2,716 were individuals lynched, most of them African American men, women, and children. In 1892, Ida B. Wells mounted a campaign to fight lynching. *See also* antilynching movement.

M

machine tools Machines used to produce other machines with standardized parts at a low cost. The development of machine tools by U.S. inventors in the early nineteenth century facilitated the rapid spread of the industrial revolution.

MAD policy *See* mutually assured destruction policy.

managed competition Government policy in the early 1990s that depended on market forces rather than government controls to reduce the cost of health insurance and medical care. This idea was the heart of the failed health-care-reform initiative proposed by President Bill Clinton (1993–2001) in the early 1990s.

manifest destiny Journalist John O'Sullivan's phrase, coined in 1845, to express the popular nineteenth-century belief that the United States was destined to expand westward to the Pacific Ocean and had an irrefutable right and God-given responsibility to do so.

manumission The act of a master liberating a slave. Virginia passed a law legalizing manumission in 1782, and various antislavery societies gained momentum in the 1780s and 1790s. Most slaveholders, however, did not willingly free their slaves. *See* abolitionism.

Marbury v. Madison An 1806 Supreme Court case that established the right of the Court to review the constitutionality of laws. The decision involved judicial appointments made during the last hours of the administration of President John Adams (1797–1801). Some commissions, including that of William Marbury, had not yet been delivered when President Thomas Jefferson (1801–1809) took office. Infuriated by the last-minute nature of Adams's Federalist appointments, Jefferson refused to send the undelivered commissions out, and Marbury decided to sue. The Supreme Court ruled that although Marbury's commission was valid and the new president should have delivered it, the Court could not compel him to do so. The Court based its reasoning on a finding that the grounds of Marbury's suit, resting in the Judiciary Act of 1789, were in conflict with the Constitution. This ruling established the concept of judicial review.

margin buying *See* buying on the margin.

market revolution Combined impact of the rapidly increasing production of goods and the development of a transportation network to distribute them. In the early nineteenth century, this led to the growth of urban production and distribution centers, western migration, and the construction of a variety of transportation methods including canals, roads, steamboats, and railroads.

maroon communities Villages of escaped African slaves established in the New World wilderness beginning in the sixteenth century. Marooners (also called outliers) typically set up communities in the undesirable swamplands of the Carolinas and Florida to avoid detection.

marriage portion Land, livestock, farm equipment, or household goods that eighteenth-century New England parents gave to their children as marriage gifts to help them start life on their own. Parents expected children to repay this gift by caring for them in their old age.

Marshall Plan The successful recovery program designed by Secretary of State George C. Marshall to restore the economies of Western Europe after World War II (1939–1945). The United States provided $13 billion in aid to sixteen nations over five years. Though Marshall invited all European nations to participate, the Soviet Union refused and demanded that its Eastern European satellites do likewise. The United States also benefited economically from the Marshall Plan. European nations spent most of their aid dollars to buy U.S. products carried on U.S. ships, and Europe's economic recovery expanded the realm of raw materials, markets, and investment opportunities available to U.S. capitalists.

Marxism A political, social, and economic movement founded in the mid-nineteenth century by the philosopher Karl Marx. Marx predicted that capitalism would fall and be replaced by a more egalitarian society of workers. Marx's ideas were later expanded by Russian revolutionary Vladimir Lenin, who criticized imperial capitalism and advocated world revolution. Marxist-Leninist ideology was behind the rise of communism in parts of the world in the twentieth century. *See also* communism.

Mason-Dixon line The surveyors' mark, mapped by Charles Mason and Jeremiah Dixon, that established the boundary between Maryland and Pennsylvania in colonial times. By the

1820s, it came to represent the division between the free North and the slave South.

mass consumption Purchasing of uniform goods created by systems of mass production beginning in the late nineteenth century. Mass consumption peaked in the years following World War II (1939–1945), when people bought a vast number of mass-produced durables from household appliances to houses.

mass production The industrial process designed to produce a great number of identical items for sale to the public on a large scale. In the late nineteenth century, most factories came to use the assembly line to maintain high volume.

McCarthyism Searching out suspected Communists and others outside mainstream U.S. society, discrediting them, and driving them from government and other employment. The term takes its name from Senator Joseph McCarthy, who gained notoriety for leading such investigations from 1950 to 1954. *See also* communism, House Un-American Activities Committee.

mechanics A class of skilled craftsmen and inventors who built and improved machinery and developed machine tools for industry in the nineteenth century. They cultivated a professional identity and established institutes to spread their skills and knowledge.

Medicare and Medicaid Health care initiatives of President Lyndon B. Johnson (1963–1969). Medicare provides the elderly with universal compulsory medical insurance financed largely through Social Security taxes. Medicaid authorizes federal grants to supplement state-paid medical care for low-income people under sixty-five. Both initiatives were passed in 1965 as amendments to the Social Security Act of 1935.

mercantilism A set of policies that regulated colonial commerce and manufacturing for the enrichment of the mother country. Mercantilist policies ensured that the American colonies in the mid-seventeenth century produced agricultural goods and raw materials to be shipped to Britain, where they would increase wealth in the mother country through reexportation or manufacture into finished goods that would then be sold to the colonies and elsewhere.

mercenary A soldier for hire who cares nothing for the motivations behind the war but will fight for either side for money.

Thousands of German mercenaries called Hessians joined the British troops during the Revolutionary War (1775–1783).

merger The voluntary combining of two or more companies to create one company. After the depression of 1893, over a thousand mergers took place. This "merger mania" was fueled largely by the finance capitalist J. P. Morgan, who hated economic competition.

mestizo Spanish for "mixed"; the offspring of white Europeans and native people, usually a white man and an Indian woman. In sixteenth-century Mesoamerica, nearly 90 percent of the Spanish settlers were men who took Indian women as wives or mistresses, resulting in a substantially mixed-race population.

Methodism A Christian revival movement characterized by open-air meetings and an emphasis on Bible study, the conversion experience ("new birth"), and devout behavior. Methodism began as an effort to reform the Church of England in the mid-eighteenth century. Methodism was integral to religious revivalism in the colonies, especially through the preaching of English minister George Whitefield. Methodism became a separate Protestant denomination after the Revolutionary War (1775–1783) and grew rapidly in the nineteenth century.

Middle Passage The brutal sea voyage from Africa to the Americas in the eighteenth and nineteenth centuries in which nearly a million Africans lost their lives. Conditions were horrific, and, on average, 15 percent of slaves died during this voyage, with mortality rates on individual ships sometimes reaching 50 percent or higher.

military-industrial complex First used by President Dwight D. Eisenhower (1953–1961) to describe the close relationship of military spending and defense contractors that emerged during World War II (1939–1945) and grew with the cold war. In the 1950s and 1960s, federal defense spending came to have a tremendous influence on the national economy, particularly in the South and West where many defense contractors were located. In his farewell address in 1961, President Eisenhower raised troubling questions about the influence of this new power in a democracy and warned the nation to be vigilant.

militia Citizens trained as soldiers who do not serve in the regular army but are called upon to assist the government during emergencies. Each of the thirteen American colonies required its citizens to enroll and train in the militia. During the Revolutionary War (1775–1783), nearly half of the colonial army was comprised of militiamen, and the U.S. Constitution gave Congress the right to call a militia to enforce the laws of the Union. The United States still maintains a militia in the form of the National Guard.

minimum wage The lowest wage that an employer may legally pay an employee. The United States passed its first minimum wage law under the Fair Labor Standards Act of 1938, part of Franklin D. Roosevelt's New Deal. Prior to this time, minimum wage laws were deemed unconstitutional.

minutemen Voluntary militia units organized by colonists in the 1770s to face British troops on short notice. These soldiers formed the core of the citizen army that met the British at the battles of Lexington and Concord.

Miranda v. Arizona A 1966 Supreme Court case that, by a vote of five to four, upheld the case of Ernesto Miranda, who appealed a murder conviction on the grounds that police had gotten him to confess without giving him access to an attorney. The *Miranda* case was the culmination of the Court's efforts to find a meaningful way of determining whether police used due process in extracting confessions from people accused of crimes. The *Miranda* decision upholds the Fifth Amendment protection against self-incrimination outside the courtroom and requires that suspects be given what came to be known as the Miranda warning, which advises them of their right to remain silent and warns them that anything they say might be used against them in a court of law. Suspects must also be told that they have a right to counsel.

miscegenation The sexual mixing of the races, especially between a white man and black woman. In slave states, despite social stigma and legal restrictions on interracial sex, it was common for slave masters to engage in liaisons with their female slaves. Many states maintained laws against miscegenation into the 1950s.

misery index A measure of economic suffering that first appeared in the 1970s. The index is calculated by adding the national unemployment rate and the average annual rate of inflation. The term reappeared during the 1996 election to underscore a healthy economy. The misery index at that time was the lowest it had been in twenty-seven years.

mission A Spanish colonial settlement in the New World. Missions were small complexes manned by priests and soldiers. The Spanish government set up missions throughout its territories in North and South America between 1500 and 1800 to lay claim to various regions and convert native peoples to Catholicism. French Jesuits and English Protestants also established missions in North America. *See also* missionaries.

missionaries Europeans or Americans of European ancestry who sought to convert Native Americans to Christianity. Jesuit priests from France and Franciscan monks from Spain both brought Catholicism to North America; Puritans from England created "praying towns" to teach Native Americans about Protestant theology. During the Second Great Awakening of the early 1800s, American Protestant missionaries established churches in Africa, India, and Hawaii. In the nineteenth century, the federal government gave $10,000 a year to missions that attempted to "civilize" Native Americans in the western territories by teaching them Euro-American agricultural techniques, gender customs, and the English language. Many Christian-based faiths in the twenty-first century, especially in the United States, still send missionaries to various parts of the world.

mixed government John Adams's 1776 plan calling for three branches of government, each representing one function: executive, legislative, and judicial. This system of dispersed authority was devised to maintain a balance of power and ensure the legitimacy of governmental procedures.

modernism An artistic style and cultural movement in the 1920s that broke with past stylistic traditions and criticized contemporary culture and values. American writers and artists of the modernist movement, many of whom made their homes in Europe, included Gertrude Stein, T. S. Eliot, F. Scott Fitzgerald, Alexander Calder, and Man Ray. *See also* Lost Generation.

money supply The amount of money circulating in the economy. The Federal Reserve, the central bank in the United States, controls the money supply. The Federal Reserve's monetary policy, or management of the money supply, determines the availability of credit. Disagreements over how to manage the money supply led to the rise of Populism in the late nineteenth century, as impoverished debtors (mostly farmers) called for expansion of the money supply through the coinage of silver. *See also* free silver.

monopoly Exclusive control and domination by a single business entity over an entire industry through ownership, command of supply, or other means. During the Gilded Age, businesses monopolized their industries quite profitably, often organizing holding companies and trusts to extract higher profits. John D. Rockefeller held a virtual monopoly of the oil refinery business in the late 1800s. *See also* Gilded Age, horizontal integration.

Monroe Doctrine The 1823 declaration by President James Monroe (1817–1825) that the Western Hemisphere was closed to any further colonization or interference by European powers. In exchange, Monroe pledged that the United States would not become involved in European struggles. Although Monroe did not back his policy with action, it was an important formulation of national goals.

Mormonism (the Church of Jesus Christ of Latter-Day Saints) The religion founded by Joseph Smith in 1830. Smith claimed he was visited by revelations and that an angel led him to golden tablets buried near his home. He translated their mysterious language in the *Book of Mormon,* which told the story of an ancient Christian civilization in the New World and predicted the appearance of an American prophet who would reestablish Jesus Christ's undefiled kingdom in America. The Mormons were deemed heretics and driven from New York to the Midwest. Smith was arrested in Illinois on charges of polygamy (the practice of a man having multiple wives) and shot dead by an angry mob in 1844. Brigham Young took over leadership and moved the people to Salt Lake City, Utah, in 1846. Utah remains the center of Mormonism in the United States. *See also* heresy.

muckrakers Journalists in the early twentieth century who exposed the corruption of big business and government. Theodore Roosevelt (1901–1909) gave them this name in reproach, borrowing the term from John Bunyan's Christian allegory *Pilgrim's Progress,* in which a character so busied himself with raking muck that he took no notice of higher things.

Mugwumps A late-nineteenth-century branch of reform-minded Republicans from Massachusetts and New York who deplored the spoils system of rewarding party loyalists with government jobs and advocated civil service reform. The name Mugwump came from the Algonquin word for "chief," but critics used the term derisively, punning that the Mugwumps straddled the fence on issues of party loyalty, "with their mug on one side and their wump on the other."

mulatto The offspring of whites and blacks. In the eighteenth- and nineteenth-century South, relationships between white male slaveholders and black female slaves often produced mulatto children. *See also* miscegenation.

multiculturalism Promoting diversity in gender, race, ethnicity, religion, and sexual preference. This political and social policy became increasingly popular in the United States during the 1970s' post–civil rights era.

multilateralism An international relations strategy in which one country partners with other countries to achieve its objectives. The strategy of multilateralism underlies such organizations as the United Nations (1945) and the North Atlantic Treaty Organization (1949).

mutually assured destruction (MAD) policy A 1950s' U.S. nuclear policy that called for a massive and unstoppable nuclear response if the Soviet Union were to launch an attack on the United States. Such nuclear reciprocation would result in the total annihilation of both countries and was thus viewed as a policy of nuclear deterrence.

N

NAACP *See* National Association for the Advancement of Colored People.

National American Woman Suffrage Association (NAWSA) Suffrage organization created in 1890 by the union of the National Woman Suffrage Association and the American Woman Suffrage Association. NAWSA played a central role in campaigning for women's right to vote.

National Association for the Advancement of Colored People (NAACP) A coalition of blacks and whites who sought legal and political rights for African Americans through the courts. Like many progressive reform coalitions, the NAACP attracted a diverse group—social workers, socialists, and black intellectuals. In the coming decades, the organization evolved from an interracial organization to a largely black organization. It played a major role in the civil rights movements of the 1950s and 1960s.

national debt Created in the late eighteenth century by the government's borrowing money from the wealthy through the sale of bonds. Alexander Hamilton believed that drawing on this source of capital to finance government would create ties of loyalty between the government and the business community.

National Labor Relations Act A law passed in 1935 that guarantees the right of U.S. workers to form unions and engage in collective bargaining (negotiate as a group with employers about wages, hours, and conditions). The National Labor Relations Act is sometimes referred to as the Wagner Act after its chief sponsor, New York Senator Robert F. Wagner.

National Woman's Party Political party originally formed as the Congressional Union for Woman Suffrage in 1913. The National Woman's Party fought for an Equal Rights Amendment to the U.S. Constitution in the early twentieth century. The group picketed the White House, conducted marches, and performed acts of civil disobedience to promote its agenda. *See also* Equal Rights Amendment.

nationalism A strong feeling of devotion and loyalty toward one nation over others. Nationalism promotes the nation's common culture, language, and customs. Politicians stirred nationalist sentiments in the American people in an attempt to garner support for the War of 1812 (1812–1814) and the Mexican-American War (1846–1848). During the 1930s, Adolf Hitler of Germany and Benito Mussolini of Italy used nationalism in demanding extreme loyalty from their people. After World War II (1939–1945), nationalism led many African and Asian colonies to demand self-government.

nativism Antiforeign sentiment in the United States that fueled a drive against immigration. In the 1920s, native-born white Protestants who viewed their own race and religion as the ideal reacted with bitter animosity to the more than 23 million immigrants who had come to the United States during the previous forty years. Many nativists, such as members of the Know-Nothing Party in the nineteenth century and the Ku Klux Klan in the twentieth century, voice anti-immigrant, anti-Catholic, and anti-Semitic sentiments.

NATO *See* North Atlantic Treaty Organization.

Navigation Acts British acts of 1650, 1651, and 1660 that, together with the Staple Act of 1663, set forth three fundamental regulations governing colonial trade. First, all colonial goods imported into England had to be transported on English ships using primarily English crews. Second, specific colonial products could be shipped only to England or to other English colonies. Third, as stipulated by the Staple Act, all goods imported into the colonies had to pass through England. The 1660 Navigation Act assessed an explicit import tax of two pence on every pound of colonial tobacco; these tobacco taxes yielded about a quarter of all English customs revenues in the 1660s. The Navigation Acts fueled tension between the colonies and the monarchy in the century leading up to the Revolutionary War (1775–1783).

NAWSA *See* National American Woman Suffrage Association.

New Deal A series of experimental social and economic programs developed by President Franklin D. Roosevelt (1933–1945) and his advisors during the 1930s in an attempt to bring the United States out of the Great Depression. These programs greatly expanded the role of the federal government and changed the way the public viewed Washington. Even though millions of Americans benefited directly from the New Deal's "alphabet soup" of agencies and programs—all known by their three- or four-letter acronyms—both relief and recovery were limited and temporary. The depression continued into the 1940s until after the country entered World War II (1939–1945), which eventually pulled the country from its economic slump.

New England   In colonial times, the English colonies of the Northeast. Today the term refers to the states of Maine, New Hampshire, Vermont, Massachusetts, Connecticut, and Rhode Island.

New Freedom   Woodrow Wilson's (1913–1921) campaign slogan from the 1912 election. "New Freedom" expressed Wilson's belief in states' rights and limited government. Wilson also railed against big business, promising to employ antitrust legislation to get rid of big corporations and give small businesses and farmers better opportunities in the marketplace. Unlike Teddy Roosevelt's (1901–1908) "New Nationalism," Wilson's program sought to revive competition rather than regulate large corporations.

New Frontier   President John F. Kennedy's (1961–1963) term for his agenda of renewed governmental activism both at home and abroad. The New Frontier focused foremost on fighting the cold war and secondarily on public service initiatives such as the Peace Corps. Although his legislative achievements were limited, Kennedy's ideas and personal appeal inspired many, especially the young.

New Left   Adopted by radical students of the 1960s and 1970s to refer to their activist movement, distinguishing themselves from the Old Left—the Communists and socialists of the 1930s and 1940s who tended to focus on labor issues rather than cultural issues. New Left students turned to grassroots organizing in cities and college campuses in their protest against the status quo and what they saw as the willingness of older generations to accommodate authority.

New Nationalism   Theodore Roosevelt's (1901–1909) campaign slogan from the 1912 election. New Nationalism expressed Roosevelt's belief in federal planning and regulation. He accepted the inevitability of big business but demanded that government act as "a steward of the people" to regulate the giant corporations. Roosevelt called for an increase in the power of the federal government, a decrease in the power of the courts, and an active role for the president. He hoped to use the government to promote social justice and democracy.

New Negro The artists and intellectuals of black America who came to prominence in the 1920s. The expression was taken from the title of an anthology of writings from the Harlem Renaissance, edited by Alain Locke. *See also* Harlem Renaissance.

new politics The shift in political campaigning from issues-based to image-based strategies, accompanied by the increasing strength of the Democratic Party. Mass media, particularly television, played a major role in this transformation during the election of 1960, when debates between John F. Kennedy and Richard Nixon were televised. The image of a young, composed Kennedy next to an older, nervous-looking Nixon proved beneficial to Kennedy, who ultimately won the presidency.

New Right The conservative political movement that achieved considerable success beginning in the 1970s. The New Right helped to elect Ronald Reagan (1981–1989) president in 1980 and enabled the Republican Party to retake both houses of Congress in the 1994 elections. New Right activists mobilized thousands of followers and millions of dollars to combat federal activism and perceived declining social morality. Though commonly associated with Christian denominations, New Right activism reached well beyond the Christian community to draw from a wide variety of demographic strata.

New South A post–Civil War vision of the South initiated by journalist Henry Grady that urged the South to abandon its dependence on agriculture and use its cheap labor and natural resources to compete with northern industry. Many southerners migrated from farms to cities in the late nineteenth century, and northerners and foreigners invested a significant amount of capital in railroads, cotton and textiles, mining, lumber, iron, steel, and tobacco in the region.

new woman A woman of the 1920s who challenged the gender roles of previous decades and demonstrated her increasing independence in such ways as working outside the home, obtaining a college education, expressing her sexuality, and becoming politically active. After suffrage was extended to women in 1920, women became more vocal on political matters but were not necessarily united in their views.

New World European name for North America, South America, and the islands of the Western Hemisphere during the Age of Exploration (1492–1600) and the subsequent period of European colonization.

new world order Political phrase first used by President Woodrow Wilson (1913–1921) following World War I (1914–1918) to encapsulate the idea that the world would no longer function as it once did. President George H. W. Bush (1989–1993) more famously used the phrase after the collapse of the Berlin Wall in 1990 to describe the dramatic changes wrought by the end of the cold war.

Niagara movement A black civil rights organization founded in 1905 by William Monroe Trotter and W. E. B. Du Bois that called for universal male suffrage, civil rights, and leadership by a black intellectual elite. The Niagara movement helped found the National Association for the Advancement of Colored People in 1909. *See also* National Association for the Advancement of Colored People.

nickelodeons Movie theaters with a five-cent admission charge that sprang up in the late 1890s. Nickelodeons peppered neighborhood streets and provided a cheap form of leisure for the working class.

nonproliferation Preventing the spread of nuclear weapons and the technology that produces them. In 1968, the United Nations approved the Nuclear Nonproliferation Treaty; in 1995, the treaty was renewed and made permanent. The treaty is designed to prevent the spread of nuclear weapons and inhibit countries with nuclear technology from aiding those without it to acquire the knowledge or the weapons themselves.

North Atlantic Treaty Organization (NATO) Post–World War II alliance formed in 1949 that joins the United States, Canada, and Western European nations into a military coalition designed to counter efforts to expand by the Soviet Union. Each NATO member pledged to go to war if any member was attacked.

Northwest Passage Rumored passageway from Europe to the Indies via the North Atlantic. From the late fifteenth through the early seventeenth century, European monarchs and trade companies sent explorers to discover such a route, which would have facilitated trade with nations in the Pacific. Explorers landed at various locales along the (now) North and South American coasts and often mistook them for India.

nullification The idea that a state convention could declare federal laws unconstitutional if they were seen to overstep congressional powers. South Carolina politicians advanced this idea in 1828 as a response to Congress's so-called Tariff of Abominations, which hurt South Carolina's already depressed cotton industry. After a heated confrontation between federal and state governments, Congress passed a more moderate tariff in 1833 that satisfied both sides. The question of federal power versus states' rights, however, was far from settled. The implied threat of nullification was secession, and the South later acted on this threat when it believed the federal government compromised its perceived right to slavery.

O

oligopoly A competitive system in which several large corporations dominate an industry by dividing the market so each business has a share of it. More prevalent than outright monopolies during the late 1800s, the oligopolies of the Gilded Age successfully muted competition and benefited the corporations that participated in this type of arrangement. This became the norm in the 1920s.

Open Door notes A document sent by U.S. Secretary of State John Hay to Japan, Russia, Germany, and France in 1899 claiming the right of equal trade for all nations that wanted to do business in China. Because it lacked colonial possessions in China, free trade was crucial to the United States to gain access to China's large markets. The Open Door notes outlined what came to be known as the Open Door policy.

outwork A system of manufacturing used in the English woolen industry; also known as "putting out." Merchants in the sixteenth and seventeenth centuries bought wool and provided it to landless peasants who spun and wove it into cloth that the merchants in turn sold in English and foreign markets.

P

pacifism The doctrine of opposition to all violent means of solving conflict. Certain religious groups, such as the Quakers, adhere to pacifism as a tenet of their faith. Pacifist techniques have also been used to bring about social change. Nonviolent disobedience was used by Mahatma Gandhi in India's struggle for independence from the United Kingdom, and Martin Luther King Jr. and many other U.S. civil rights leaders adopted Gandhi's approach to battle segregation and discrimination during the 1950s and 1960s. During the 1960s and early 1970s, pacifists led the opposition to the Vietnam War (1957–1975).

Paleo-Indians People who began migrating to North and Central America between 15,000 and 13,000 BP, ancestors of modern American Indians. Many archaeologists believe that Paleo-Indians came from Asia by crossing a land bridge called Beringia that once connected Siberia and Alaska. *See also* Clovis people.

Pan-Americanism The notion of a community of North and South American countries. Secretary of State James Blaine called the first Pan-American conference in 1881, which his successor cancelled later that same year. When Blaine returned to the post of secretary of state in 1889, he scheduled a new Pan-American conference, but little came of it other than a minor Washington organization called the Pan-American Union. The United States soon lost South America's goodwill when the United States invaded Chile in 1891 in retaliation for a riot against U.S. sailors in Valparaiso.

party An organized political body with specific ideologies or interests, established with the goal of organizing the electorate and directing the policies of a government. While not part of the Constitution, competitive political parties appeared quickly in the United States during the election of 1796 and have been maintained ever since.

patent A government document granting an inventor the rights to the production, use, and sale of his or her invention for a given number of years. Congress issued its first Patent Act in 1790.

paternalism The idea that slavery was a set of reciprocal obligations between masters and slaves, with slaves providing labor and obedience and masters providing basic care and necessary guidance. The concept of paternalism denied that the slave system was brutal and exploitative. While paternalism did provide some protection against the worst brutality, it did not guarantee decent living conditions, reasonable work, or freedom from physical punishment.

patriarchy A gendered power structure in which men rule autocratically over women, either as heads of families or as rulers of society. This term has also been applied to government leaders who rule autocratically over their subjects. During the Revolutionary War (1775–1783), patriots accused the British monarch of patriarchy toward the American colonists.

patriotism Devotion to one's homeland and a willingness to sacrifice on its behalf. Governments often appeal to patriotic leanings to rally citizens' support, as the U.S. government did especially aggressively during World War II.

patronage The power of elected officials to grant government jobs to party members to create and maintain strong party loyalties. In the United States, patronage was first used extensively by Martin Van Buren in early-nineteenth-century New York.

peaceful coercion Thomas Jefferson's (1801–1809) strategy to force the British and the French to accept the rights of the United States as a neutral nation. In response to offensive actions taken against U.S. ships, Jefferson forbade exportation of goods to Europe. His policy, articulated under the Embargo Act of 1807, hurt the U.S. economy more than it did those of the French and British. Though the Embargo Act was rescinded in 1809, tensions continued over America's neutral rights, leading eventually to the War of 1812 (1812–1814).

peaceful coexistence Used by Premier Nikita Khrushchev of the Soviet Union in 1956 to call for diminished tensions between capitalist and communist nations in the cold war. As a sign of the reduced hostility, Khrushchev and Vice President Richard Nixon exchanged official visits.

peasant A farm laborer who often worked land held by a landlord. In Europe, these laborers sometimes owned or leased a small plot in the town and worked collectively with other village laborers on the landlord's land. The majority of immigrants to the New World were peasants seeking a better life and land of their own.

peonage (debt peonage) Policy of using debt as a pretext for forced labor. As cotton prices declined during the 1870s, many sharecroppers fell into permanent debt and merchants conspired with landowners to exploit their labor. *See also* sharecroppers.

perestroika The policy introduced by Soviet president Mikhail Gorbachev during the 1980s that referred to economic restructuring. Gorbachev's policies during his presidency contributed to the freeing of Eastern Europe from Soviet domination and led, unintentionally, to the 1991 breakup of the Soviet Union. *See also glasnost.*

perfectionism Christian movement of the 1830s that believed people could achieve moral perfection in their earthly lives because the Second Coming of Christ had already occurred. Perfectionism attracted thousands of followers, particularly New Englanders who had settled New York.

personal-liberty laws Laws passed by northern legislatures in the 1850s to challenge the federal Fugitive Slave Act, which required that northerners return escaped slaves to their southern masters. These diverse statutes included such measures as noncooperation laws and the prohibition of using state officials to catch runaways.

phalanxes Utopian cooperative work groups of the 1840s that organized as part of the Fourierist movement in which all members were shareholders in a community as an alternative to capitalist wage labor. Most phalanxes did not last more than two or three years. *See also* Fourierism.

pietism A Christian revival movement characterized by Bible study, the conversion experience ("new birth"), and devout behavior; began as an effort to reform the German Lutheran Church in the mid-seventeenth century. German pietist immigrants were integral to religious revivalism in the middle colonies in the mid-eighteenth century and shared convictions similar to the Methodists. *See also* Methodism.

Pilgrims One of the first Protestant groups to come to America, seeking a separation from the Church of England. They founded Plymouth, the first permanent community in New England, in 1620. *See also* separatists.

planters Owners of large farms (called plantations) that were worked by twenty or more slaves. Planters had accrued a great deal of local, statewide, and national political power in the South by 1860, despite the fact that they represented a minority of the white electorate in those states. Planters' dominance of southern politics demonstrated their success at convincing white voters that the slave system benefited all whites, even those without slaves.

Plessy v. Ferguson An 1896 Supreme Court case in which African American Homer Plessy challenged a Louisiana law that required segregation on trains passing through the state. After ensuring that the railroad and the conductor knew that he was of mixed race (Plessy appeared to be white but under the racial code of Louisiana was classified as "colored" because he was one-eighth black), he refused to move to the "colored only" section of the coach. The Court ruled against Plessy by a vote of seven to one, declaring that "separate but equal" facilities were permissible according to section 1 of the Fourteenth Amendment, which calls upon the states to provide "equal protection of the laws" to anyone within their jurisdiction. Initially, the decision was viewed as a victory for segregationists, but in the 1930s and 1940s, civil rights advocates referred to the doctrine of "separate but equal" in their efforts to end segregation. They argued that segregated institutions and accommodations often were not equal to those available to whites and finally succeeded in overturning *Plessy* in *Brown v. Board of Education* in 1954. *See also Brown v. Board of Education.*

pocket veto Presidential means of killing a piece of legislation without issuing a formal veto. When congressional Republicans passed the Wade-Davis bill in 1864 (which required that 50 percent of residents in the former confederate states take a loyalty oath before returning to the Union), Abraham Lincoln (1861–1865) used the pocket veto to kill the legislation by simply not signing it and letting it expire after Congress adjourned.

police action A military action undertaken without a formal declaration of war by regular armed forces against perceived violators of international peace. This term was applied to the participation of U.N.-authorized troops in the Korean War against Communist North Korea in the early 1950s.

political machine A highly organized nineteenth-century political group, often compared to new technological innovations because of its efficiency and complexity. Most machines developed within major cities and were run by a boss who had influence over elected officials. Politicians within a machine provided services or favors for their constituents in exchange for votes, sometimes resulting in their being brought up on charges of bribery or corruption. New York City's Democratic Party machine, called Tammany Hall, dominated the politics of that city for over a century. *See also* Tammany Hall.

poll tax Fee required in order to vote. Poll taxes were used throughout the South to prevent freedmen from voting after the Civil War (1861–1865). Northern states also used poll taxes to keep immigrants and others deemed unworthy from the polls.

polygamy The practice of a man having multiple wives. Polygamy was adopted by some male Mormons in the mid-nineteenth century, which created great national controversy. The federal government outlawed the practice in 1890.

pool An illegal arrangement made between business leaders in an industry to set prices above a certain level. Pools, used for centuries to avoid ruinous competition, were largely replaced by mergers in the late nineteenth century. *See also* merger.

popular sovereignty The pre–Civil War idea that the residents of a territory should determine, through their legislatures, whether to allow slavery. Michigan senator and Democratic presidential candidate Lewis Cass introduced this solution to the problem of slavery in the territories in 1848. Senator Stephen A. Douglas of Illinois gave the policy its name in the Kansas-Nebraska Act of 1854.

Populism The late-nineteenth-century political movement of farmers, most notably in the West and South, that identified laissez-faire capitalism (in which the government has limited involvement) and big business as responsible for the worsening economic circumstances in rural America. In 1892, the People's (or Populist) Party captured a million votes and carried four western states, representing the first agrarian protest to truly challenge the entrenched two-party system. *Populism* has come to mean any political movement that advocates on behalf of the common person, particularly for government intervention against big business.

Powell doctrine The military strategy articulated by Colin Powell, chairman of the Joint Chiefs of Staff, during the Persian Gulf War (1991). It advocated that the United States use military force only as a last resort and in cases when national security was directly threatened. When used, force should be swift and overwhelming and accompanied by both a clear exit strategy and strong public support.

pragmatism   A philosophy that judges ideas by their consequences and concerns itself with solving contemporary problems rather than seeking ultimate truths. Developed in the early twentieth century by psychologist William James, pragmatism was embraced by progressives. *See also* progressivism.

praying towns   Christianized Native American settlements supervised by New England Puritans in the seventeenth and eighteenth centuries.

predestination   The Christian belief that God possesses complete knowledge of the future, including who will and will not be saved. Predestination invalidated the idea that salvation could be obtained through good works and was a fundamental tenant of Puritan theology. *See also* Calvinism.

Presbyterianism   The Protestant Christian denomination in which church government is run by elected assemblies (presbyteries) rather than by congregations (congregationalism) or bishops (the episcopal system). Presbyterianism adhered closely to the teachings of John Calvin and differed from Congregational Puritanism and other Calvinist denominations primarily in government structure. *See also* Calvinism, Puritanism.

preservationists   Early-twentieth-century activists who fought to protect the natural environment from commercial exploitation, particularly in the West. Preservationists notably established many national parks such as Yosemite, Sequoia, and King's Canyon in California.

price revolution   The high rate of inflation in Europe in the mid-1500s. This inflation resulted from the introduction of New World Spanish wealth into the European economy, which doubled the money supply in Europe. The price revolution brought about profound social changes by reducing the political power of the aristocracy and leaving many peasant families on the brink of poverty, setting the stage for a substantial migration to North America.

primogeniture   An inheritance practice by which a family's estate was passed on to the eldest son, forcing many younger children into poverty. In the Revolutionary era, republican Americans increasingly felt this was unfair. As a result, most state legislatures rejected the practice by passing laws requiring the equal distribution of estates among offspring.

profiteering Unethical means of making business profits, especially by companies that profit by raising prices during national emergencies (such as wars and natural disasters).

progressivism A wide-ranging twentieth-century reform movement that advocated government activism to mitigate the problems created by urban industrialism. The movement rejected the fatalism of earlier social thought in analyzing social problems and replaced it with empirical social science and a belief in administrative efficiency. Progressivism reached its peak in 1912 with the creation of the Progressive Party, under whose banner Theodore Roosevelt (1901–1909) ran for president. *Progressivism* has come to mean any general effort advocating for social welfare programs.

prohibition The law dictated by the Eighteenth Amendment of the Constitution that banned the manufacture and sale of alcohol in the United States. Prohibition took effect in January 1920, but public resistance was intense. Speakeasies (illegal saloons) sprang up around the country, and bootleggers (illegal alcohol providers) supplied alcohol smuggled from Canada and Mexico. Organized crime invested heavily in bootlegging, and gang-war slayings generated much publicity. Public pressure led to the repeal of prohibition by the Twenty-first Amendment in 1933.

Promontory Point The site in Utah where the railway lines built by the Union Pacific and Central Pacific met in 1869, completing the first transcontinental railroad line. A golden spike was driven into the track at that point to commemorate the historic event. *See also* transcontinental railroad.

propaganda The spreading of ideas that support a particular cause. Although propaganda does not always distort facts, it usually misrepresents the views or policies of one's opponents. During World War I (1914–1918), the U.S. Committee on Public Information, led by George Creel, published literature and sponsored speeches to increase public hostility toward Germany and therefore garner support for U.S. involvement in the war.

proprietary colony A colony created through the grant of land from the English monarch to an individual or group, who then set up a form of government largely independent from royal control. Maryland, the Carolinas, New Jersey, New York, and Pennsylvania were all established as proprietary colonies.

proprietors   In seventeenth-century Puritan society, those who determined how the land of a township would be distributed. To guarantee a wide distribution of property, the General Courts of Massachusetts Bay and Connecticut gave the title of a township to a group of proprietors and allowed them to distribute land among the settlers.

Protestantism   The Christian movement that separated from the Roman Catholic Church in sixteenth-century Europe during the Reformation. Protestants criticized the Catholic practices of following the pope and praying to saints because they believed that only Jesus Christ should serve as the intermediary between God and mortals. They urged a return to simpler worship services, paid close attention to the teachings of Scripture, and believed that people could not be instrumental in their own salvation. Some of the first English settlers of the United States, such as the Pilgrims and the Puritans, were Protestants escaping religious persecution. *See also* Catholicism, Reformation.

public virtue   Willingness to set the public good above private desires. This term gained popularity during the Revolutionary era and was viewed as the foundational principle of republican government.

pump priming   First used during the Great Depression of the 1930s to describe the government's practice of generating economic activity by pouring money into the financial and industrial systems; also known as deficit spending.

Puritans   A Christian sect in post-Reformation England that believed the Church of England needed to purify its practices, namely by eliminating lingering elements of Catholicism ("popery"). Puritans did not want to separate from the Church of England but rather to reform it from the inside. Many Puritans left for the New World in the seventeenth century to establish purified religious communities and were instrumental in founding Massachusetts and Connecticut. Puritans embraced the Calvinist doctrine of predestination and believed in righteous conformity among their members. *See also* Calvinism, Reformation.

Q

Quakers A Christian sect, also called the Society of Friends, that began in mid-seventeenth-century England. Quakers rejected formal theology and an educated clergy and instead embraced the guidance of an inner light, bestowed upon them by God. Believing that everyone was capable of achieving salvation, they adhered steadfastly to principles of social equality and pacifism and were actively involved in American reform movements, especially abolition.

R

racism The belief that one race is superior to another, often leading to prejudice and discrimination against the allegedly inferior race. In the United States, racism most often suggests a white bias against people of other races, but it is not restricted to this connotation. Sociologists distinguish between individual and institutional racism. Individual racism refers mainly to the prejudicial beliefs and discriminatory behavior of individuals in relations to other ethnic groups. Institutional racism refers to the policies that restrict the opportunities of minorities in communities, schools, businesses, and other areas. Affirmative action policies were adopted by many U.S. institutions in the late twentieth century in an effort to combat institutional racism. *See also* affirmative action.

radical Reconstruction Policies of the radical Republicans in the South following the Civil War (1861–1865). Carpetbaggers (Northern Republicans working in the South), scalawags (Southern Republicans), and newly freed blacks worked to restore the southern economy, reviving agricultural production, building roads, and creating schools for black children. For the first time, blacks participated fully in civic life. Southerners largely disapproved of the former slaves' active participation in society, however, and vigilante organizations such as the Ku Klux Klan used violence to drive blacks (and all other Republicans) from the polls. Weakened by southern opposition and their own escalating corruption, radical Republican governments collapsed soon after they began.

radical Whigs Eighteenth-century opposition party in the British Parliament that challenged the cost of the growing British empire and the subsequent increase in tax collector positions that were used for patronage. They demanded that British government include more representatives of the propertied classes. The political opinions of the radical Whigs were welcomed by American colonists who resented the heavy taxes imposed upon them. *See also* Whigs.

ratification The approval of important federal documents such as the Articles of Confederation and the Constitution (as well as all subsequent amendments) by state legislatures. While the Articles of Confederation required unanimous consent of the state governments for ratification, the Constitution required ratification by only nine of thirteen colonies. Ratification also refers to the approval of national treaties by Congress.

Reaganomics describes (often derisively) the supply-side economic policies of President Ronald Reagan (1981–1989). *See also* supply side.

recession A decline in overall business activity. If a recession spreads nationwide, the country suffers from a drop in buying, selling, and production, and a rise in unemployment. When U.S. companies began to relocate to other countries in search of cheaper labor and production, the resulting deindustrialization prompted a severe recession in the United States in 1975 and 1976.

Reconstruction The period between 1865 and 1877 in which newly freed slaves, abolitionists, and Republican politicians attempted to make changes in the South that would ensure political equality for the freedmen and grant them greater economic rights. The Reconstruction Act of 1867 divided the South into five military districts until new state constitutions were drafted. All eleven Confederate states were readmitted to the Union by 1870. Reconstruction, however, faded with the withdrawal of troops from the South. The Democratic Party soon dominated the South, and blacks lost all political gains made under Reconstruction.

Red scare The fear of communism that swept the country first after World War I (1914–1918) and again after World War II (1939–1945). The first Red scare led to a series of government raids on alleged subversives. While the government did not find evidence of revolutionary conspiracies, it suppressed civil liberties in the spirit of preemption. Public institutions joined the crusade, with libraries removing politically controversial books from circulation and schools firing unorthodox teachers. The police shut down radical newspapers, and state legislatures refused to seat elected representatives who professed socialist ideas. The Red scare lost its momentum after the government failed to uncover any real menace. It emerged again, however, after World War II, when cold war fears amplified the threat of communism.

Red-baiting Attempting to discredit individuals or ideas by associating them with communism. This was a common tactic during the Red scares following World War I (1914–1918) and World War II (1939–1945). *See also* Red scare.

Redeemers Ex-Confederates who sought to return the political and economic control of the South to white Southerners in the decades after the Civil War (1861–1865). They believed that Union support of the freedmen had deprived the South of democratic self-government and organized secret societies and campaigns of terror to regain it, leading to the undoing of Reconstruction.

redemptioner A type of indentured servant, common in the Middle Colonies in the eighteenth century. Unlike other indentured servants, redemptioners did not sign a contract before leaving Europe. Instead, they found employers after arriving in America.

reform Darwinism A social theory, based on Charles Darwin's theory of evolution, that emphasized activism, arguing that humans could speed up evolution by altering the environment. A challenge to social Darwinism, reform Darwinism condemned a laissez-faire approach to economy—one in which the government does not interfere—and demanded that the government take a more active approach to solving social problems. It became the ideological basis for progressive reform in the late nineteenth and early twentieth centuries.

Reformation The Christian reform movement that began in 1517 with Martin Luther's critiques of the Roman Catholic Church and led to the formation of a new Christian sect called Protestantism. The English Reformation began with Henry VIII's break with the Catholic Church in 1534. The Church of England soon became the official English church, from which many American denominations descended. *See also* Baptist, Calvinism, Church of England, Congregationalism, Methodism, Presbyterianism.

relocation centers Internment camps to which Japanese Americans were sent during World War II (1939–1945), when the United States was at war with Japan. Despite the fact that no Japanese American was ever charged with espionage, over 100,000 people, many of them native-born U.S. citizens, were forcibly moved to these relocation centers in isolated areas of the western states. In 1988, the U.S. government issued a formal apology and $20,000 to each of the surviving prisoners.

reparations Efforts, usually by a government, to make up for harm or wrongdoing that has occurred in the past. Reparations often come in the form of money payments or the return of property to individuals or groups. Other forms include apologies or changes in governmental policies. After World War I

(1914–1918), the Allies—headed by the United States, France, Great Britain, and Italy—required Germany to pay vast sums for expenses incurred during the war, which triggered further German discontent. In 1988, the U.S. government agreed to pay $20,000 per person to Japanese Americans who had been held in internment camps during World War II (1939–1945). Since the end of the Civil War (1861–1865), various groups have called for the government to pay reparations to the descendants of slaves.

republic A state without a monarch and with a representative system of government. Revolutionary leaders in eighteenth-century America sought to found a republic as an antidote to the corruption they saw in the British monarchy.

republican motherhood The idea that American women's moral superiority gave them a special role to play in the new political and social system. In the early to mid-nineteenth century, republican mothers were to instill the values of patriotic duty and republican virtue in their children and mold them into exemplary American citizens with moral and religious education.

Republican Party One of the two major political parties of the United States, the other being the Democratic Party. The Republican Party began as an antislavery organization in 1854, welcoming as members anyone who opposed the extension of slavery into the western territories. Abraham Lincoln (1861–1865) was the first Republican president, and Republicans were influential in the abolition of slavery and women's suffrage. In the later half of the twentieth century, Republican ideology began to shift to the right, and in the twenty-first century the Republican Party is seen as the more conservative of the two major parties, emphasizing states' rights, a strong military presence abroad, and moral values. *See also* Democratic Party.

republicanism A form of government in which supreme power resides in the hands of voting citizens and is exercised by a representative government answerable to this group of voters. In Revolutionary-era America, republicanism became a social philosophy that reacted against European-style monarchy, embodied a sense of community, and called individuals to act for the public good. Many northern white Americans in the early 1800s ascribed to "democratic republicanism," which emphasized equality in both politics and family life.

requerimiento A Spanish colonial document that conquistadors were commanded to read, beginning in 1514, to all native peoples they encountered in their colonization of the New World. The *requerimiento* offered the Indians peace and freedom if they would covert to Christianity, and war and enslavement if they refused. There was little chance that Indians would understand a document read in Spanish even if they had wished to convert, and the *requerimiento* was used largely as a justification for conquest.

reservations Federal territories given to American Indians beginning in the 1860s in an attempt to reduce tensions between Indians and western settlers. Most tribes did not relocate willingly to reservations but rather moved under governmental force. The Sioux War and Nez Perce War were two of many conflicts that erupted over reservation relocations in the late nineteenth century.

Restoration The name given to the reign of Charles II, King of England, the monarch whom Parliament crowned in 1660 following a decade of Puritan rule under Oliver Cromwell. Charles II's ascension to the throne prompted many Puritan followers of Cromwell to immigrate to the New World.

restrictive covenant A limiting clause in a real estate transaction intended to prevent the sale or rental of property to classes of the population considered "undesirable," such as African Americans, Jews, or Asians. Such clauses were declared unenforceable by the Supreme Court decision in *Shelley v. Kraemer* (1948) but continued to be used informally in spite of the ruling.

revenue sharing The return of federal tax money to the states for their use. President Richard Nixon (1969–1974) sought to reverse the concentration of power in Washington by initiating a decentralization of governmental functions in 1972, and revenue sharing was a part of this process.

reverse discrimination Discrimination against whites or males. In the wake of the civil rights and feminist movements of the mid-twentieth century, when affirmative action mandates increased the number of minorities and women in the workplace and at educational institutions, some felt that diversity came at the expense of equally or better-qualified whites and males. *See also* affirmative action.

Roaring Twenties *See* Jazz Age.

robber barons A group of industrialists who dominated U.S. social, political, and economic life in the late nineteenth century.

During this period, the unregulated nature of industrial capitalism favored the rise of competitive risk takers who employed questionable tactics such as labor exploitation and shady stock market deals to amass their fortunes.

rock and roll A style of popular music, influenced by country-and-western music and black rhythm and blues. White rock and roll performers such as Elvis Presley dramatically increased its popularity with white audiences in the 1950s.

Roe v. Wade A 1973 Supreme Court case that found, by a vote of seven to two, that state laws restricting access to abortion violated a woman's right to privacy guaranteed by the due process clause of the Fourteenth Amendment. The decision was based on the cases of two women living in states with stringent anti-abortion laws, Texas and Georgia. Citing the individual rights of both women and physicians, the Court ruled that the Constitution protects the right to abortion and that states cannot prohibit abortions in the early stages of pregnancy. Critics argued that since abortion was never addressed in the Constitution, the Court could not claim that legislation violated fundamental values. They also argued that since abortion was a medical procedure with an acknowledged impact on a fetus, it was inappropriate to invoke the kind of "privacy" argument that was used in *Griswold v. Connecticut* (1965), which dealt with the right to obtain contraception. Defenders suggested that the case should be argued as a case of gender discrimination, which did violate the equal protection clause of the Fourteenth Amendment. Others said that the right to privacy in sexual matters was indeed a fundamental right.

Roosevelt Corollary to the Monroe Doctrine The 1904 assertion by President Theodore Roosevelt (1901–1909) that the United States would act as a "policeman" in the Caribbean region and intervene in the affairs of nations that were guilty of "wrongdoing or impotence" in order to protect U.S. interests in Latin America. Roosevelt was referencing an 1823 declaration by President James Monroe (1817–1825) that European nations would no longer be allowed to establish colonies in the Western Hemisphere. *See* Monroe Doctrine.

Royal colony A colony ruled directly by the English monarch or his representatives. By 1700, most of the proprietary colonies in North America had come under royal control. *See also* proprietary colony.

S

salutary neglect British colonial policy during the reigns of George I (r. 1714–1727) and George II (r. 1727–1760) that relaxed supervision of internal colonial affairs and contributed significantly to the rise of American self-government.

scab Someone who works in place of a striking worker; also called a strikebreaker. The origin of the term dates to 1777, when it meant someone who refused to join a guild or labor organization. In 1877, the U.S. federal government protected scab train crews in the great railroad strike.

scalawag A southern white who joined the Republicans during Reconstruction and was viewed as a traitor by ex-Confederates. Scalawags included wealthy ex-Whigs and yeomen farmers who had not supported the Confederacy and who believed that an alliance with the Republicans was the best way to attract northern capital to the South and thereby improve the weak southern economy.

Schenck v. United States A 1919 Supreme Court case ruling unanimously that Congress had the right to protect the public against speech that had the possibility of inciting panic. During World War I (1914–1918), Charles Schenck and other members of the Socialist Party printed and mailed out flyers urging young men who were subject to the draft to oppose the war in Europe. In upholding the conviction of Schenck for publishing a pamphlet urging draft resistance, Justice Oliver Wendell Holmes established the "clear and present danger" test for freedom of speech. Such utterances as Schenck's during a time of national peril, Holmes wrote, could be considered the equivalent of shouting "Fire!" in a crowded theater. Although Holmes later modified his position to state that the danger must relate to an immediate evil and a specific action, the "clear and present danger" test laid the groundwork for those who later sought to limit First Amendment freedoms. The current standard for determining the bounds of free speech is the "imminent lawless action" test, established by the Court in 1969, meaning that the First Amendment does not protect a speaker who prompts other people to do harm or commit a crime when those people are likely to engage in a lawless action.

scientific management A system of organizing work developed by Frederick W. Taylor in the late nineteenth century.

Scientific management was designed to get the maximum output from the individual worker and reduce the cost of production, using methods such as the time-and-motion study to determine how factory work should be organized. The rigid structure of the system was never applied in its totality in any industry, but it contributed to the rise of the efficiency expert and the field of industrial psychology. Labor resisted this effort because it de-skilled workers and led to the speedup of production lines. Taylor's ideas were most popular at the height of the Progressive Era. *See also* Taylorism.

SCLC *See* Southern Christian Leadership Conference.

Scott v. Sandford An 1857 Supreme Court case ruling that no black person, enslaved or free, could claim citizenship rights. The case was brought before the Court on behalf of Dred Scott, a slave from Missouri, who had briefly lived with his master in Illinois and Wisconsin, two territories that forbade slavery on the basis of the Missouri Compromise of 1820. Scott sued for his own and his family's freedom on the grounds that he had lived in free territory. Five of the nine justices were from the South and seven were Democrats, and, reflecting the bitter political divisions at the time, the Court voted seven to two to return Scott to his master. The justices also took the opportunity to declare that Congress could not prohibit slavery in the U.S. territories and that the Missouri Compromise was unconstitutional. The decision was highly controversial and brought the nation closer to civil war.

secession A state's withdrawal from the Union. Embittered over Abraham Lincoln's election and perceived northern threats to the slave system, eleven southern states left the Union between 1860 and 1861. South Carolina seceded first, followed by Mississippi, Florida, Alabama, Georgia, Louisiana, Texas, Virginia, Arkansas, Tennessee, and North Carolina. Four slave states in the Upper South (Missouri, Kentucky, Maryland, and Delaware) stayed loyal to the Union.

Second Continental Congress *See* Articles of Confederation.

Second Great Awakening The widespread Christian religious revivals of the early nineteenth century. By the 1820s, these "camp meetings" had spread to the Atlantic seaboard states, finding especially enthusiastic audiences in western New York and Pennsylvania. The outdoor settings permitted huge attendance, which itself intensified the emotional impact of the experience. Ministers adopted an emotional style and invited an immediate experience of conversion and salvation. More women than men initially were attracted to the religious revivals; women then recruited their husbands and sons to join them. Church membership doubled in the United States between 1800 and 1820, much of it among evangelical groups such as Methodists, Baptists, and Presbyterians.

secondary labor boycott A technique used by unions during a strike in which a second party's support is enlisted to pressure the primary target to accept union demands. A secondary labor boycott was used in the Great Pullman Boycott of 1894 in which Pullman workers appealed to American Railway Union members, who in turn refused to operate sleeping cars owned by George M. Pullman. Pullman cut his workers' wages during an economic panic but refused to lower the rents on company housing.

second-wave feminism *See* feminism.

sectionalism Concern only for the interests of one part of a country, typically one's own. While sectionalism is most often used to describe the divided loyalties of the North and the South, it can also be used to describe other regions of the country.

segregation The practice of separating people of different races (typically blacks and whites) either through law or cultural precedent. In 1881, Tennessee passed the first segregation law, which separated railroad passengers by race. The Supreme Court enabled other states to follow Tennessee and established legal segregation when it declared the Civil Rights Act of 1875, which had outlawed segregation in many public accommodations, unconstitutional in 1883. The Supreme Court upheld legal segregation in *Plessy v. Ferguson* (1896) when it declared that facilities for blacks and whites could be separate as long as they were of equal quality. This decision set a major precedent that stood until the Court ruled against segregation in *Brown v. Board of Education* (1954). *See also* Jim Crow, *Brown v. Board of Education, Plessy v. Ferguson.*

selective service *See* draft.

self-made man A middle-class icon based on the ideal that hard work, temperate habits, and honesty in business was the key to prosperity for individuals. This ideal became a central theme of American popular culture in the nineteenth century.

sentimentalism The European-spawned idea that emphasized emotions and physical appreciation of God, nature, and other people, over reason and logic. Sentimentalism had an impact on Americans starting in the early nineteenth century, as love became as important a consideration in marriage as financial standing.

"separate but equal" doctrine *See Plessy v. Ferguson.*

separate spheres A concept of gender relations that developed in the Jacksonian era and continued well into the twentieth century, holding that women's proper place was in the private world of hearth and home (the private sphere) and men's was in the public world of commerce and politics (the public sphere). The doctrine of separate spheres eroded slowly over the nineteenth and twentieth centuries as women became more and more involved in public activities. *See also* cult of domesticity.

separation of church and state A phrase used by Thomas Jefferson in a letter to the Danbury Baptist Association in 1802. Jefferson wrote, "I contemplate with solemn reverence that act of the whole American people which declared that their legislature should 'make no law respecting an establishment of religion, or prohibiting the free exercise thereof,' thus building a wall of separation between church and state." Jefferson was quoting the First Amendment, which prevented the federal government—what he called the state—from creating laws about religion. This amendment, however, did not constrain individual states from endorsing a particular church and thus restricting the activities of other churches. *See also* disestablishment.

separatists Christian religious groups that sought to separate from the Church of England. One of the first Protestant groups to emigrate to America was a separatist group: the Pilgrims, who settled Plymouth Colony in 1620 in what is now Massachusetts. They believed that the Church of England was hopelessly corrupt and formally separated from it, which resulted in their persecution and precipitated their departure from England. In this way they differed from the Puritans, who thought that by setting up pious religious communities in America they could, by example, lead the Church of England back to righteousness.

Shakers A religious group derived from the Quakers that followed the visions of "Mother Ann" (Ann Lee), a cook from Manchester, England, who advocated celibacy, work, and simplicity. The Shakers were persecuted in England in the mid-eighteenth century and emigrated to New York, where they established both a church and a utopian community. Shaker communities spread throughout the Northeast, welcoming both blacks and whites and operating under an ideal of sexual equality. The Shakers reached their height of 6,000 members in the 1840s and declined thereafter.

sharecropping A labor system developed during Reconstruction by which freedmen agreed to work the land and pay a portion of their harvested crops to the landowner in exchange for land, a house, and tools. A compromise between free blacks and white landowners, this system developed in the cash-strapped South because the freedmen wanted to work their own land but lacked the money to buy it, while the white landowners needed agricultural laborers but did not have money to pay wages.

silent majority The segment of U.S. society to whom President Richard Nixon (1969–1974) appealed—the "unblack, unpoor, and unyoung." President Nixon first used the term derived from the title of a book by Ben J. Wattenberg and Richard Scammon, in a 1969 speech when he described those who supported his positions but did not publicly assert their voices as did those involved in the anti-war, civil rights, and women's movements.

sit-in A nonviolent protest tactic first popularized by African American college students seeking civil rights in the South. In 1960, four black students took seats at the whites-only lunch counter of a Greensboro, North Carolina, store, intending to "sit in" until they were served, and their actions prompted the desegregation of the lunch counter. As protests in the 1960s spread beyond civil rights, many radical groups adopted the sit-in as their method of activism, occupying businesses and institutions that discriminated against them.

slash and burn agriculture A method of farming used by Indians throughout North and South America before the arrival of Europeans. Indians commonly cut down and burned forested areas to clear land for crops, allowing the tree ash to nourish the soil. They then repeated the process in new areas after exhausting the soil. European settlers adopted the process and used it throughout the colonial period until the development of commercial fertilizers enabled them to practice a more sustainable method of agriculture.

slave power A suspected conspiracy of southern politicians and their northern business allies to expand slavery into new territories. Antislavery advocates popularized this theory in the 1850s, causing both black and white Northerners to believe that their personal liberty was in danger.

smallpox A highly contagious viral disease that was brought to the New World by Europeans, killing a large number of native inhabitants. Smallpox also ravaged British and American troops during the Seven Years' War (1756–1763) and the Revolutionary War (1775–1783), often proving more dangerous than the enemy, although both sides in the Revolutionary War were able to inoculate some of their soldiers—purposely giving them a mild form of the disease to protect them from the full-fledged version. English physician Edward Jenner first developed a more reliable, safer smallpox vaccine in 1796, but the disease continued to exist throughout the world until the 1940s, when a better vaccine was created. Scientists believe that in the 1900s alone, smallpox killed more than 300 million people worldwide. The last U.S. case of smallpox occurred in 1949.

SNCC *See* Student Nonviolent Coordinating Committee.

social Darwinism A social application of Charles Darwin's biological theory of evolution by natural selection, or survival of the fittest. This late-nineteenth-century theory encouraged the notion of human competition and opposed government intervention in the natural human order. Social Darwinists justified the increasing inequality of late-nineteenth-century industrial U.S. society as natural. They claimed that reform was useless because the rich and poor were precisely where nature intended them to be and believed that intervention would slow the progress of humanity.

social gospel movement A religious movement in the late nineteenth and early twentieth centuries founded on the idea that Christians have a responsibility to reform society. The movement encouraged adherents to put Christ's teachings to work in their daily lives by actively promoting social justice.

social purity movement Progressive reform movement of the late nineteenth and early twentieth centuries that aimed to rid cities of vice, particularly prostitution. To end the "social evil," as reformers referred to prostitution, the social purity movement combined ministers who wished to stamp out sin, doctors concerned about the spread of venereal disease, and women reformers determined to fight the double standard that made it acceptable for men to engage in premarital and extramarital sex but punished women who strayed. Together this group waged campaigns to close red-light districts in cities across the country and lobbied for the Mann Act, passed in 1910, which made it illegal to transport women across state lines for "immoral purposes."

Social Security Act An important welfare policy of the New Deal designed to provide a modest income for the elderly. The Social Security Act (1935) required that pensions for the elderly be funded not by direct government subsidies but instead by tax contributions from workers and their employers. Although this provision subtracted money from consumption, it gave contributing workers a personal stake in the system and made it politically viable. Social Security created unemployment insurance (paid for by employers' contributions) that provided benefits for workers who lost their jobs. It also issued multimillion-dollar grants to the states to use to support dependent mothers and children, public health services, and the blind.

socialism A governing system in which the government, or state, owns and operates the largest and most important parts of the economy. Socialism in the United States reached its peak during the Great Depression, when the Communist Party—which embraced socialist ideals—counted around 100,000 members. Many conservatives accused President Franklin D. Roosevelt's (1933–1945) New Deal of advocating socialism, but Roosevelt claimed his policies were designed to strengthen capitalism— in which private individuals own the means of production— even though they greatly expanded the federal government's role in private life.

socialized medicine A label applied by the American Medical Association in the early 1950s in a campaign against Harry S. Truman's (1945–1953) recommendation that a federally underwritten national health care system be enacted. The attempt to link Truman's program with leftist politics was successful in arousing congressional and public opinion against the plan.

Society of Friends *See* Quakers.

solid South The tendency of southern states to vote overwhelmingly for Democratic candidates after the Civil War (1861–1865) until the 1960s, when opposition to Democratic civil rights measures prompted them to turn to the Republican Party.

Sons of Liberty Carefully directed groups of protesters that sought to channel popular discontent against British rule, terrorizing local British officials and other symbols of colonial authority in the decade of hostilities leading up to the American Revolution (1775–1783). They fought acts that imposed unfair taxes on colonists and were the primary participants in the Boston Tea Party.

Southern Christian Leadership Conference (SCLC) A civil rights organization. After the Montgomery bus boycott (1955–1956) Martin Luther King Jr. and other civil rights leaders formed the SCLC in 1957 to coordinate civil rights activity in the South. King was chosen as the first leader of the organization and remained the head until his assassination in 1968.

southern strategy A political strategy used by the Republican Party to win votes by appealing to southern voters on the basis of cultural issues. This strategy was first used in the 1960s to attract voters opposed to civil rights reforms and has since centered around issues such as abortion, religion, and taxes.

Spanish flu *See* influenza.

speakeasies Illegal saloons that sold alcohol to the public during prohibition in the 1920s. At the speakeasies, men and women drank bootleg (illegally provided) liquor, listened to jazz music, and danced the Charleston and other new steps. Since speakeasies were often associated with organized crime, many social critics viewed them as places of corruption, sin, and general debauchery.

specie Gold or silver coins used by banks to back paper currency. In the early nineteenth century, most U.S. money consisted of notes and bills of credit, which were redeemed on demand with specie by the Second Bank of the United States.

speculator Someone who enters a market to buy and then resell at a higher price with the sole goal of making money. The nineteenth-century western land market was dominated by people who acquired land at a low price through political influence and then sold it for a profit to settlers.

sphere of influence A geographical area beyond a nation's borders over which it claims control. The Soviet Union's domination of Eastern European countries after World War II (1939–1945) extended the Soviet sphere of influence dangerously close to the U.S. sphere of influence, in Western Europe.

spoils system An arrangement in which party leaders reward party loyalists with government jobs. This slang term for *patronage* comes from the adage "To the victor go the spoils." Widespread government corruption during the Gilded Age spurred reformers to curb the spoils system through the passage of the Pendleton Act in 1883, which created the Civil Service Commission to award government jobs on the basis of merit.

Square Deal Theodore Roosevelt's (1901–1909) domestic reform program that called for government control of corporate abuses. In one of his first acts as president, Roosevelt ordered his attorney general to begin a secret antitrust investigation of the Northern Securities Company, a company that monopolized railroad traffic in the Northwest and symbolized corporate high-handedness to small investors and farmers. The Supreme Court held that Northern Securities violated the Sherman Antitrust Act of 1890 and ordered its dissolution. Following this success, Roosevelt initiated investigations into dozens of other trusts during his first term in office and used his rallying cry of a "square deal" for both labor and capital as a campaign slogan in the 1904 election. *See also* antitrust, monopoly.

squatter Someone who settles on land he or she does not own. Many eighteenth- and nineteenth-century settlers established themselves on land before it was surveyed and entered for sale, requesting the first right to purchase the land when sales began.

stagflation An economic term coined in the 1970s to describe the condition in which inflation and unemployment rise at the same time.

Stamp Act The British law of 1765 that taxed all paper used for colonial documents, such as wills, newspapers, and pamphlets. The Stamp Act was designed simply to raise money for the king and affected nearly everyone, falling hardest on businesses and lawyers. It required that a special stamp be affixed to colonial documents to prove the tax had been paid. Many colonists objected vociferously to the Stamp Act, and protest erupted throughout the colonies. Parliament rescinded the Stamp Act in March 1776 due to economic considerations but followed it with the Declaratory Act, which asserted that Parliament had a right to legislate for the colonies "in all cases whatsoever."

state sovereignty A state's autonomy or freedom from external control. The federal system adopted at the Constitutional Convention in 1787 struck a balance between state sovereignty and national control by creating a strong central government while leaving the states intact as political entities. The states remained in possession of many important powers on which the federal government cannot intrude.

states' rights An interpretation of the Constitution that argues that the states hold the ultimate sovereignty and have power over the federal government. Expressed in the Virginia and Kentucky Resolutions of 1798, the states' rights philosophy became the basis for resistance by the South against federal attempts to control slavery.

steam engine   A significant invention of the industrial revolution that harnessed mechanical energy from high-pressure steam. Steam engine technology spread rapidly throughout Europe and the United States beginning in the late eighteenth century and was particularly important to improving the efficiency of the railroad and shipping industries.

strict constructionism   An approach to constitutional law that attempts to adhere to the original intent of the writers of the Constitution. Strict construction often produces Supreme Court decisions that defer to the legislative branch and to the states and restricts the power of the federal government. Justice Hugo Black was one of the most forceful proponents of the doctrine. In *Reid v. Covert* (1957), he wrote that the "United States is entirely a creature of the Constitution." Broad constructionism allows for different interpretations of the Constitution according to the current political climate of the nation and the values of the justices presiding at that time.

strike   A protest tactic in which laborers refuse to work in an effort to bargain with employers for better working conditions. Strikes became a common strategy of labor unions during the industrial revolution in the 1800s and early 1900s and continue to be employed in the twenty-first century. Common striking actions include neglecting to attend work, picketing outside the workplace, or occupying the workplace without performing work (a "sit-down" strike.)

strikebreaker   *See* scab.

Student Nonviolent Coordinating Committee (SNCC)
A student civil rights group that began in the 1950s under the mentorship of activist Ella Baker. SNCC initially embraced an interracial, decentralized, and nonhierarchical structure that encouraged leadership at the grassroots level and practiced the civil disobedience principles of Martin Luther King Jr. As violence toward civil rights activists escalated and black protest extended from the South to the entire nation in the 1960s, SNCC changed its direction. It expelled nonblack members and promoted "black power" as its new rallying cry. Members abandoned King's philosophy of peaceful resistance for the teachings of Malcolm X, who condoned violence as self-defense.

subsidy Government funds used to support production or consumption of a good. Governments subsidize domestic farmers and other manufacturers to produce goods deemed important for a country's well-being when the free market would not support such production. Government subsidies also lower the price of certain goods so that more consumers can afford them. Subsidies are controversial because they interfere with the free market and especially with international trade.

subtreasury system A scheme under which the federal government would provide localized banking functions for farmers, allowing them credit and marketing opportunities not controlled by private firms. This banking reform was promoted by the Populist Party in the late nineteenth century.

suburbanization The movement of the upper and middle classes beyond city limits to less crowded areas with larger homes, connected to city centers by public transportation. By 1910, 25 percent of the population lived in these new communities. The 2000 census revealed that the majority of Americans lived in the suburbs.

suffrage The right to vote. In the early national period, suffrage was limited by property restrictions. Gradually state constitutions gave the vote to all white men over the age of twenty-one. Over the course of U.S. history, suffrage has expanded as barriers of race, gender, and age have fallen. The term *suffrage* is most often associated with the efforts of U.S. women to secure voting rights. The Nineteenth Amendment, which secured suffrage for women, became part of the Constitution in 1920. In 1965, Congress passed the Voting Rights Act, which upheld the Fifteenth Amendment and outlawed the various voting restrictions southern states had placed on African American suffrage.

suffragists Those (mostly female) who were active in seeking voting rights for women in the nineteenth and early twentieth centuries, believing that suffrage was an inherent right for all individuals.

Sun Belt The southern and southwestern regions of the United States that grew tremendously in industry, population, and influence after World War II (1939–1945).

Sun Dance A Sioux ceremony in which an entire tribe celebrated the rites of coming of age, fertility, the hunt, and combat. The ritual involved four days of fasting and dancing in supplication to Wi, the sun.

superpower A post–World War II term used to describe a country capable of exerting global power. During the cold war, between 1945 and 1990, the United States and the Soviet Union were referred to as the world's two superpowers. After the fall of the USSR in 1991, only the United States maintained the title.

supply-side economics An economic theory based on the premise that tax cuts for the wealthy and for corporations will stimulate the economy by encouraging investment and production, thus creating more jobs, generating more taxable income, and increasing government revenues. Embraced by the Reagan administration (1981–1989) and other conservative Republicans, this theory reversed Keynesian economic policy, which assumed that the way to stimulate the economy was through federal spending on public works and general tax cuts that put more money into the hands of ordinary people.

sweatshop A small, often poorly ventilated room, used for the production of clothing beginning in the later nineteenth century. As mechanization transformed the garment industry with the introduction of foot-pedaled sewing machines and mechanical cloth-cutting knives, independent tailors were replaced with workers (mostly women and children) hired by contractors to sew pieces of cloth into clothing. Sweatshops proliferated in U.S. cities to accommodate this garment work.

syndicalism A radical political ideology advocating that labor unions control government and industry and distribute benefits equally within a given trade. This approach was endorsed by the Industrial Workers of the World at the start of the twentieth century.

syphilis A sexually transmitted disease contracted by Christopher Columbus's sailors through sexual encounters with New World women and unwittingly carried back to Europe, where it may already have had a foothold.

T

Tammany Hall The most notorious political machine of the nineteenth century, located in New York City and run by Democrat William Marcy "Boss" Tweed. The excesses of the Tweed ring (such as expensive bribes made at the taxpayers' expense) led to a clamor for political reform. Tweed fled to Europe in 1871 to avoid prosecution but was eventually convicted and died in jail. *See also* political machine.

tariff A tax on imports designed to raise revenue for the government and protect domestic products from foreign competition. A hot political issue throughout much of U.S. history, in the late nineteenth century the tariff became particularly controversial as Republicans, who viewed it as a protective system, and Democrats, who were free traders by tradition, made the tariff the centerpiece of their political campaigns.

task system A system of labor in which a slave was assigned a daily task to complete and allowed to do as he wished upon its completion. This system offered more freedom than the gang-labor system, in which slaves worked set hours under careful supervision. The task system was used throughout the slave South before the Civil War (1861–1865), but it was most common in the rice-growing regions of South Carolina.

Taylorism A business strategy popular in the early twentieth century and championed by efficiency expert Frederick W. Taylor. Taylorism emphasized standardization of production through such innovations as the assembly line. Industrial leaders used Taylor's methods of scientific management not only to increase productivity but also to de-skill labor, transferring control of the work process from workers to managers. The changing nature of work lay behind much of the labor unrest of the late nineteenth and early twentieth centuries. *See also* scientific management.

teach-in University gatherings in the 1960s where the political, diplomatic, and moral aspects of the nation's involvement in Vietnam were debated.

technocrat An elite bureaucrat or leader who attains power through knowledge of technology, economics, or science rather than through democratic means. Such politicians hope to modernize their countries but do not necessarily consider the impact on the people they rule. In the late twentieth century, the term also became associated with private business, as executives made the decision to outsource or automate aspects of corporations without considering the impact on existing employees.

telecommuters People who perform their jobs at home with the use of electronic communication devices such as computers, modems, and faxes. Telecommuting became common in the 1990s as the growth and development of the Internet and World Wide Web revolutionized communications.

telegraph Revolutionary mid-nineteenth-century technology that used an electrical wire to transmit messages over a long distance. Between 1844 and 1861, nearly all major cities from Boston to San Francisco were wired for the telegraph. With the successful construction of a transatlantic cable linking the United States and Europe in 1866, the telegraph was also used by the federal government to monitor international affairs. Though Samuel F. B. Morse is often credited with inventing the telegraph, it grew from a body of scientific knowledge gradually acquired by a number of scientists. Morse applied the discoveries of others to create his machine, which he patented in 1840. His communications code—the "Morse code"—became the universal language of the telegraph.

temperance movement A reform movement to end drunkenness that urged people to abstain from the consumption of alcohol. Begun in the 1820s, this movement achieved its greatest political victory with the 1919 passage of the Eighteenth Amendment prohibiting the manufacture, sale, and transportation of alcohol. That amendment was repealed by the Twenty-first Amendment in 1933.

tenements High-density, cheap, five- or six-story housing units built in the late nineteenth century and designed for large urban populations. In the United States, tenements were constructed in the northern urban centers to house the burgeoning immigrant and later African American populations in the late 1800s and early 1900s. New York City's tenements in particular were known for their severe overcrowding and lack of ventilation and plumbing.

third world First used in the late 1950s during the cold war to describe newly independent countries in Africa and Asia that were not aligned with either Communist nations (the second world) or non-Communist nations (the first world). Later, the term was applied to all poor, nonindustrialized countries, in Latin America as well as in Africa and Asia. Many international experts see *third world* as a problematic category when applied to such a large and disparate group of nations, and they criticize the discriminatory hierarchy suggested by the term.

third-wave feminism *See* feminism.

time-and-motion study An engineer's study of an industrial task that determined the most efficient method for producing the greatest amount in the least amount of time. Factories then set this time as the standard to which workers were expected to conform. Time-and-motion studies became popular in the late 1800s and early 1900s. Frederick W. Taylor conducted a series of such studies while working for a Philadelphia steel company in the 1880s. He later published his studies in 1911 as *The Principles of Scientific Management. See also* scientific management, Taylorism.

tobacco A staple crop of the southern American colonies first produced commercially in Virginia in 1612 and essential to the British empire's economy and to the colony's success. Despite its being a luxury item with no industrial purpose that many believed was harmful to health and family life, tobacco flourished. Production and distribution improved and expanded quickly, leading to falling prices and decreased profits beginning in the 1640s. Colonists continued to produce tobacco but also turned to other crops, such as cotton, rice, and sugar.

Tory *See* loyalist.

total war The style of warfare in which one nation mobilizes the whole of its resources against the entirety of another nation to destroy its ability to wage war. The Civil War (1861–1865), World War I (1914–1918), and World War II (1939–1945) all employed strategies of total war.

town meeting The political process in colonial New England in which the town's inhabitants and freemen elected selectmen and other officials who administered local affairs. Town meetings offered a level of popular participation unprecedented in the seventeenth century. Almost every adult male could speak out and vote, although the same privileges were not extended to women. Many New England towns still hold town meetings, thus maintaining the most direct form of democracy in the United States.

trade deficit The importation by a nation of more than it exports. Contributing to the economic problems of the 1970s, the United States posted its first trade deficit in more than a century as the emerging industrial economies of Germany and Japan began to provide stiff international competition.

trade slaves A small proportion of unfree West Africans who were sold from one African kingdom to another and were not considered members of the society that had enslaved them. European traders began buying trade slaves from African princes and warlords in the early sixteenth century.

transcendentalism A nineteenth-century intellectual movement that believed individuals should look within themselves for truth and guidance rather than conform to the dogmas of formal religion. In many ways, transcendentalism represented less an alternative to the values of mainstream society than an exaggerated form of the rampant individualism of the age. Proponents included intellectuals such as Ralph Waldo Emerson, Henry David Thoreau, and Margaret Fuller.

transcontinental railroad The means of transportation that connected the eastern United States with the state of California and other territories in the West. President Abraham Lincoln (1861–1865) signed the Pacific Railroad Act in 1862, which outlined the plan to create the railroad. The two companies hired to lay the tracks, Union Pacific and Central Pacific, completed the line in Promontory, Utah, on May 10, 1869. The transcontinental railroad contributed to the development of the Great Plains and the integration of the western territories into the rest of the Union.

trench warfare A battle strategy common during the Civil War (1861–1865) and World War I (1914–1918) in which armies fought each other with firearms from fortifications—trenches—dug within the ground. Technological advances, especially in tanks, outmoded trench warfare as a viable strategy following World War I.

triangle trade Three-way trade, especially between Europe, the New World, and the west coast of Africa in the seventeenth, eighteenth, and nineteenth centuries. Common items exchanged in the triangle trade included sugar, tobacco, cotton, alcohol, fish, lumber, fur, and slaves.

trickle-down economics *See* supply-side economics.

Truman Doctrine   President Harry S. Truman's (1945–1953) assertion that U.S. security depended on stopping any Communist government from taking over any non-Communist government—even nondemocratic and repressive dictatorships—anywhere in the world. Beginning in 1947 with U.S. aid to help Greece and Turkey stave off Communist pressures, this approach became a cornerstone of U.S. foreign policy during the cold war.

trusts   Large business mergers in the late nineteenth and early twentieth centuries. These combinations became a problem because their size allowed them to inhibit competition and control the market for their products. *See also* antitrust.

Turner thesis   The opinion offered by historian Frederick Jackson Turner at the 1893 Columbian Exposition in Chicago, arguing that the existence of a frontier (a borderland between European and native settlement) shaped American identity. Turner feared that westward expansion had eroded the frontier and that, without it, America would lose the high drama of struggle that made it unique.

U

U-boats German submarines, first used during World War I (1914–1918). Germany threatened to use their new weapon against British ships and those of Britain's allies, a threat acted on when a U-boat sank the British luxury liner *Lusitania* off the coast of Ireland in 1915. The deaths of 128 Americans on board created an uproar in the United States, causing some newspaper editorials to call for entering the war against Germany.

UFW *See* United Farm Workers.

unicameral legislature A one-house assembly in which the elected legislators directly represent the people. Considered efficient and democratic, this type of assembly was established in Pennsylvania during the American Revolution (1775–1783). After the Revolution, the U.S. governmental system developed a bicameral legislature, represented by the House of Representatives and the Senate.

unilateralism An international relations strategy in which one country pursues its objectives individualistically. In the early 2000s, the United States was accused of acting in a unilateral nature in its invasion of Iraq. Though a coalition of over thirty nations did support the United States in its efforts, a number of key international nations abstained. More importantly, the U.S. military action did not have the sanction of multilateral institutions, such as the United Nations and the North Atlantic Treaty Organization.

unions Organizations of workers that began during the industrial revolution to secure rights from employers, such as wages, hours, and benefits. In the United States, skilled workers began forming organizations in the early 1800s to obtain better pay. In the mid-1800s, national labor unions began emerging, and in 1881, a group of labor leaders formed the Federation of Organized Trades and Labor Unions of the United States and Canada. Five years later, it reorganized as the American Federation of Labor. *See also* American Federation of Labor-Congress of Industrial Organizations.

Unitarianism A religious movement that went against Calvinist doctrines emphasizing human sinfulness and rejected the belief in the Holy Trinity—or God in three parts: Father,

Son, and Holy Ghost—held by most Christians, choosing instead to believe in the oneness of God. In America, Unitarianism developed in the 1700s within the Congregational churches of New England, maintaining the idea that each congregation should govern itself. It officially separated from Congregationalism with the creation of the Unitarian Universalist Association in 1825. *See also* Congregationalism.

United Farm Workers (UFW) A union of farm workers founded in 1962 by Cesar Chavez and Dolores Huerta. The UFW sought to empower the mostly Hispanic migrant farm workers who faced discrimination and exploitative conditions, especially in the Southwest.

Upper South The eight northernmost southern states. During the Civil War (1861–1865), four of the Upper South states (Arkansas, North Carolina, Tennessee, Virginia) joined the Confederacy and the other four (Delaware, Kentucky, Maryland, and Missouri) remained in the Union.

urban liberalism An early twentieth-century reform movement organized by unions and politicians who sought state measures to improve the life of the working class of the cities.

urban renewal A reform movement of the 1950s and 1960s in which city planners, politicians, and real estate developers leveled urban tenements and replaced them with modern construction projects. These new high-rise housing projects, however, weakened community bonds and led to an increase in crime.

urbanization The process in which a population shifts from a predominately rural society to a predominately urban society. Industrial growth in the years following the Civil War (1861–1865) brought about a massive redistribution of population. Cities expanded rapidly, with New York, Chicago, and Philadelphia boasting populations of more than a million by the turn of the century. Urban growth resulted both from internal migration and immigration, and cities teemed with diverse populations—poor laborers and millionaires, middle-class managers and corporate moguls, blacks and whites, immigrants and the native born. Townhouses, tenements, and new apartments buildings competed for space with skyscrapers and large department stores, while ball fields, amusement arcades, and public libraries provided the city masses with recreation and entertainment. For all the benefits of city life, it also came with a darker side, as the close proximity of diverse groups led to increased racial, ethnic, and class tensions.

utopias Communities founded by reformers and transcendentalists to help realize their spiritual and moral potential and to escape from the competition of modern industrial society. The most famous communal experiment was Brook Farm, founded by the transcendentalists outside of Boston in 1841.

V

vaudeville A professional stage show composed of singing, dancing, and comedy routines that changed live entertainment from its seedier predecessors like minstrel shows to family entertainment for the urban masses. Vaudeville became popular in the 1880s and 1890s, the years just before the introduction of movies.

vertical integration A system in which a single person or corporation controls all processes of an industry from start to finished product. Andrew Carnegie first used vertical integration in the 1870s, controlling every aspect of steel production from the mining of iron ore to the manufacturing of the final product, thereby maximizing profits by eliminating the use of outside suppliers or services.

veto The power of the president and state governors to unilaterally reject legislative bills. Unlike the absolute veto that still exists in the United Kingdom, held by the prime minister, the U.S. president has limited veto power. Congress may override a presidential veto with a two-thirds majority vote. In 1996, Congress approved a law that gave the president a line-item veto, the ability to veto individual items without vetoing the whole bill. In 1998, the Supreme Court ruled the law unconstitutional.

vice-admiralty courts Military tribunals composed only of a judge with no local common-law jury. The Sugar Act of 1764 required that offenders be tried before this tribunal rather than in local courts, provoking opposition from smugglers accustomed to acquittal before sympathetic local juries.

Victorianism Mid- and late-nineteenth-century culture during the long reign of Queen Victoria in Great Britain and those countries under its influence, including the United States. Victorianism championed moral reform, justice, and social responsibility in a time of great economic and social upheaval.

Vietnam syndrome The opposition to U.S. military involvement in overseas conflict. The term was used by political conservatives to criticize what they saw as passive U.S. foreign policy in the last quarter of the twentieth century. Such critics believed that the failure of the Vietnam War (1957–1975) led to reluctance to intervene in other areas of the world.

Vinland The name given by Vikings to an area of the North American coast, somewhere between Newfoundland and Cape Cod, Massachusetts, that they briefly settled around 1000 AD, The Vikings, from what is now Norway, were the first Europeans to reach the continent, five hundred years before Christopher Columbus.

virtual representation The notion propounded by British Parliament in the eighteenth century that the House of Commons represented all British subjects, wherever they lived and regardless of whether they had directly voted for their representatives. Prime Minister George Grenville used this idea to argue that the Stamp Act (1765) and other parliamentary taxes on colonists did not constitute taxation without representation. American colonists rejected this argument, insisting that political representatives derived authority only from explicit citizens' consent indicated by elections, and that members of a distant government body were incapable of adequately representing their interests.

W

wage slavery Used by critics of capitalism to suggest that working-class wage laborers occupied a position analogous to chattel slaves. Unlike chattel slaves, however, wage workers could quit their jobs and, in theory, better their condition. The term became increasing popular with Marxist and Socialist criticism of industrialization in the mid- to late nineteenth and twentieth centuries.

War Democrats A faction of the northern opposition party during the Civil War (1861–1865) that opposed emancipation but backed a policy of continuing to fight because they wanted to maintain union of the states.

War Hawks Young Republicans elected to the U.S. Congress in the fall of 1810 who were eager for war with England to end impressments (compulsory military service) and avenge foreign insults.

War on Poverty The political initiative of President Lyndon Johnson (1963–1969) concerned with using government programs to reduce national poverty. The Economic Opportunity Act of 1964 was the first major response to the War on Poverty. It helped impoverished youth with programs like Head Start (a preschool program for poor children) and work-study grants and allocated money to businesses willing to hire the long-term unemployed. Most controversially, it encouraged poor communities to form their own organization. Poverty did decline in the 1960s, but it declined mostly for the elderly and male-headed families. Some liberals argued that the only real solution to poverty was a redistribution of income, a measure that was never part of Johnson's plan. Johnson relied on a combination of government programs and overall economic prosperity to improve the poor's standard of living. The economy, however, never increased enough to enable such a victory. Johnson conceded this much, but insisted that "no one would ever again be able to ignore the poverty in our midst."

ward The basic unit of municipal government in the late nineteenth century. City councils were made up of representatives from these districts, and it was through the ward system that the urban political machine operated.

wars of national liberation Leftist movements rebelling against colonial or oligarchic governments in the third world. In the 1960s, the United States saw many of these struggles as attempts to extend the reach of Soviet communism, while the Soviet Union saw them as legitimate struggles for freedom and national self-determination.

welfare capitalism The idea that a capitalistic, industrial society can operate benevolently to improve the lives of workers. The notion of welfare capitalism became popular in the 1920s as industries used scientific management to improve safety and sanitation in the workplace and instituted paid vacations and pension plans.

welfare state A nation that provides for the basic needs of its citizens, including such provisions as old-age pensions, unemployment compensation, child care facilities, education, and other social policies. Unlike the major European countries, such provisions appeared in the United States only with the coming of the New Deal in the 1930s. *See also* New Deal.

westward expansion Americans' settlement westward, particularly in the nineteenth century. Westward movement increased rapidly in the 1840s. Until then, the overwhelming majority of Americans lived east of the Mississippi River, but by 1850 the boundaries of the United States stretched to the Pacific and the nation had more than doubled its size. The nation's revolution in transportation and communication, its swelling population, and its booming economy propelled the westward surge. Westward expansion was not without cost, however, as it led to bloody wars with both the native populations and the Spanish as well as conflicts over where to permit slavery.

Whigs In the United States, a political party that began in 1834 with the opponents of Andrew Jackson (1829–1837), who they thought was treating the presidency like a monarchy. They took their name from a British political party with a reputation for supporting liberal principles and reform. The British Whigs rose in power during the Glorious Revolution of 1688 and favored "mixed government" in which the House of Commons would have a voice in shaping policies, especially the power of taxation, as opposed to a monarchy. The Whig Party in the United States dissolved in the 1850s when the question of whether to extend slavery to the territories divided them.

white collar Middle-class professionals who are salaried workers as opposed to business owners or wage laborers. White-collar workers first appeared in large numbers during the industrial expansion in the late nineteenth century. Their ranks were composed of lawyers, engineers, and chemists as well as salespeople, accountants, and advertising managers. Unlike blue-collar workers, so named for their traditionally blue work uniforms, white-collar workers performed a minimum of manual labor and so were often expected to dress more formally.

X

xenophobia Fear of foreigners and foreign cultures, often leading to the hostile treatment of immigrants. *See also* nativism.

Y

yellow journalism Newspapers that specialize in sensationalistic reporting. The name came from the ink used to print the first comic strip to appear in color, in William Randolph Hearst's *New York Journal* in 1895. Yellow journalism is generally associated with the inflammatory reporting leading up to the Spanish-American War (1898).

yellow-dog contract The policy in which a worker, as a condition of employment, promises not to join a union. Employers in the late nineteenth century used this along with the blacklist and violent strikebreaking to fight unionization of their workforces.

yeoman A farmer who owned a small plot of land sufficient to support a family, tilled by family members and perhaps a few servants. Thomas Jefferson envisioned a nation based on democracy and a thriving agrarian society, built on the labor and prosperity of the yeomen. In the southern states, yeoman farmers, as opposed to southern slaveowning planters, were the norm on the eve of the Civil War (1861–1865).

Z

zoot suit An oversized suit of clothing in fashion in the 1940s, particularly among young male Mexican Americans. In June 1943, a group of white sailors and soldiers in Los Angeles, seeking revenge for an earlier skirmish with Mexican American youths, attacked anyone they found wearing a zoot suit. The violence lasted for days and was later known as the zoot suit riots.